Left Behind

Little Girl Left Behind

Sheena Harrison

With Linda Watson-Brown

**SIMON &
SCHUSTER**

London · New York · Sydney · Toronto · New Delhi

A CBS COMPANY

First published in Great Britain by Simon & Schuster UK Ltd, 2012
A CBS COMPANY

1 3 5 7 9 10 8 6 4 2

Simon & Schuster UK Ltd
1st Floor
222 Gray's Inn Road
London WC1X 8HB

www.simonandschuster.co.uk

Simon & Schuster Australia, Sydney
Simon & Schuster India, New Delhi

A CIP catalogue record for this book
is available from the British Library.

ISBN 978-0-85720-961-0

Typeset in Fournier by M Rules
Printed and bound by CPI Group (UK) Ltd, Croydon, CR0 4YY

While this book gives a faithful account of the author's experiences,
some names, places and dates have been changed to protect
the privacy of the individuals involved.

Contents

Mummy

I love to see the aeroplanes. When the sun shines, I lie on the grass outside the cottage where I live with my Granny Morag. I squirm in the sunshine, with the warm blades tickling my sun-kissed skin. The jets make a loud noise but I don't put my hands over my ears like some of the other children do; I love the sound, I wouldn't want to block it out for a second, because it gives me hope.

I can hear all of my family inside the house, all of my uncles and aunties, making a noise, talking to each other, talking over each other. I've been brought up with them as if they are my brothers and sisters. None of them are, not really, but it's a big, raggle-taggle sort of family, and I get a bit confused about who's who. There's always noise and the house is always full of people.

But someone is missing.

My mummy.

I know who she is and I never get confused about her. I know that she isn't here and I know that my heart aches for her.

Mummy left for America last summer when I was three years

old – but I know she'll come back one day. She promised me she would. She promised me that she would find us a beautiful house and build a new life for us across the sea. I don't know where America is but I know it's very far away. I can't just go to see her on the bus. She doesn't live in one of the cottages near to us on the farm where our house is. We never bump into her when we go to the shops or for a walk. America is, I know, very, very far away.

To get there, my mummy went away in an aeroplane just like the ones I love to watch, so when I lie on the ground I try to just think of her. I try to ignore the tears falling from my eyes, and the pain that hurts me all over. It's hard to do that, because my body is always sore, but if I can get through, if I can just concentrate on Mummy, it will all be fine.

With every plane that passes over, I get a little sadder. I'm only four now, and she's been gone for a year, and there have been so many planes. None of them have brought Mummy yet. I wonder when I'll see one of them and it will be the one which has her inside? I'm a little confused about how it might happen, but I think that my mum will just jump out when the plane passes over our house. I hope she doesn't hurt herself when she lands. I hope she lands gently. Maybe she'll fall onto the grass beside me and I'll give her a great big cuddle so that she feels better just in case she has hurt herself.

I wonder whether it hurts a lot, jumping out of a plane? More than anyone, I know that you can put up with a huge amount of pain. There are times when I think I can't hurt any more, times when I think I will split open from the agony I feel, but it passes.

If she breaks her leg or her arm when she jumps out of the plane to get to me, I'll make her better. I'll hug her and kiss her, and she'll be happy because we'll have each other.

Once I've helped Mummy, I know she'll help me. I dream that she will take me inside and we'll pack all of my things, all of the lovely clothes that she has been sending me since she left. We'll gather them all together and then she'll take my hand. When we say goodbye to Granny Morag and everyone else, they won't be able to stop us, because my mummy will be there. She'll look after me, she'll protect me and she'll make all the bad things stop.

I really want the bad things to stop.

I've wanted that for a while now, but it seems that wanting it on my own isn't enough. I need a grown-up to help me, but none of the grown-ups in my life seem to notice. That's because they say I'm a bad girl. They say that I tell lies; that I make up stories. They say that no one should believe a word I say and that, if I'm not careful, I'll get people into trouble. So, they say, I should keep quiet.

But I'm not a bad little girl, truly, I'm not.

I hope that Mummy will see that I'm a good girl. I'm not what Granny Morag says I am. I'm not a liar. I don't make things up. As I think about this, about the things I'm called, I can't help the hot tears from running down my face. I'm lying on my back, so they quickly drip down the sides of my cheeks and land in my hair and my eyes sting in the bright sunshine. I don't want to sit up. I don't want to tear my gaze away from the bright blue which holds the promise of Mummy.

Sometimes I have to watch for an awfully long time before a plane passes and then I hold my breath, desperately waiting to see if she will fall out of the sky and into my world. I think she'll float like an angel. Maybe she'll wear a dress like a fairy or a princess, and it will sparkle in the sun as she slowly reaches me, then she'll wrap me up in her love and hold me tight for ever.

But the planes fly past and my mummy doesn't fall out of any of them. The sky gets darker and the grass gets damp as the day draws to a close. I can hear Granny Morag shouting at me and I know that I have to go inside. Another day has ended and nothing has changed. Maybe she'll come tomorrow; maybe she's getting ready to leave America right now.

I hold the thin sliver of hope to my heart and close my eyes as I walk indoors. Deep inside, I wonder whether she'll ever save me. But I have to believe. I need something to hold on to in the middle of the hell I call my life. I know it must happen. I need to trust that it will . . . but when?

When will Mummy come home?

Chapter 1

Falling in love

I 've had to piece together the early years of my life from the words of a woman who hated me and another who deserted me. The story of how I came to be was generally agreed upon by both of them, but they presented different versions of the details. For my mother, it was a story of love and passion, of betrayal and cruelty. For my granny, it was a tale of loose morals and stupidity, a mistake with lasting consequences that had been made by many girls in the past and will be repeated by plenty in the future.

In the middle there was me. I know that both of the women who played such a part in my life had their own reasons for what they said to me, but I also know that I didn't get the full story from either of them. My mother and grandmother obviously had history long before I came on the scene, and I think that my existence just cranked up whatever had happened between them for those years. I expected certain things from each of them, but I was caught in the middle of everything. Just a little lost girl who became a victim of an ongoing feud between two women who should have protected her. I wouldn't be here if it wasn't for them. Their blood runs through my veins, and they have made me who I am, but they have also left me with so many questions unanswered and so many regrets. We all have to make sense of who we are, we find our own place in our families (no matter how dysfunctional those families are), and we become a combination of what has been given to us as an accident of birth and what we do with our lives. I've always been piecing my life together because there have been parts of it missing for as long as I can remember. There is evidence for some of it; I can access birth and marriage certificates, I can work out who lived where at what point, but I can't really find a reason for some of the things which happened to me, and which were *allowed* to happen to me, so I stick to the stuff that is documented, and try to build on that as I wonder how to make sense of my own life.

My mother was the first of Granny Morag's ten children. Her name was Kathleen and she was born in the late 1930s in a little farming village in Scotland, south of Edinburgh. Morag's first husband – my mum's father – had died of heart failure and her first five children were born to him. She then met her second husband, Big Kenny, and had another five bairns. I never knew my biological granddad but I loved Big Kenny as if he was blood to me. He was a good man, gentle and kind – very different from his wife in every way. I don't have any details about how they got together but, knowing my granny, I'd imagine that she engineered it all. In fact, I wouldn't be surprised if she just turned up at Big Kenny's door one morning with a wedding ring and the banns in her hand, telling him to get a move on or he'd be late for his own wedding! He was an easy-going soul and had no desire for anything in life except for a full belly, warm feet, and a harmonious household. He didn't do too badly with the first two, but there was no chance of an easy life with Morag around.

They lived in a cottage on the farm where the whole family worked. There were four linked cottages and, when I was little, everyone was crammed into one tiny living space. It beggars belief to think of two adults and ten children in there at one time, but that was simply how poor people lived in those days. They were grateful to have a job, and grateful to have a house which came with that job. They worked hard and life was difficult, but they got on with things. That isn't to say that there weren't casualties – there certainly were, but there was little time for emotion or sensitivity back then.

Granny Morag was never a woman to be crossed. She was as tough as old boots and I suspect she informed Kenny as to how their marriage was going to work. She was a little woman, with dark hair pulled back into a 'bun' and a look on her face which implied that life was a terrible disappointment and that she had suspected as much all along.

She had two sides though. She could be kind, she could be warm, but it's her temper and her bad side that stick in my mind, not the rare moments of big-heartedness or charity. She'd had a hard life – and I would find out so much more about that hardship as I got older – but living on the land, which was a difficult world for anyone, brought that hard side of her nature to the fore.

Mum's family weren't farmers, but farm labourers. Like so many others in the 1940s and 1950s, they gave their lives to the land but got very little in return. Their homes were tied to the job

and they worked all hours of the day to make money for someone else. Mum hated it. She hated the smell and the lifestyle. She
hated the scrabbling to make ends meet and the dirt which got
into everything. I've heard her story from lots of different
sources – including some of it from her – but it's clear that she
never wanted to become the next generation's version of her own
mother. The daily grind, the constant cleaning, the poverty, the
lack of opportunity and choice were not things that attracted my
mum. She wanted more and, although she would have to start
small, she planned to have a very different life to that of the
woman who gave birth to her.

When she was sixteen, Kathleen left for the city. Edinburgh
held lots of promise for a young girl, and there were plenty of
opportunities even for someone with no qualifications and no
contacts. The Scottish capital was bustling, full of tourists and
businesses, and Mum soon got a job in the kitchen of a huge
hotel. She was anonymous while she was there, just another
country girl looking to make a new life for herself as best she
could. She tried so hard to achieve something. I know that she
enjoyed her job, and enjoyed the freedom that came with it. She
loved the excitement and bustle of the city and could be whoever
she wanted to be away from the farm.

At weekends she would return home to her huge family,
often trying to play matchmaker by taking one of her co-
workers with her, and seeing if they would take a shine to any
of her unmarried brothers. Her own love life was non-existent
until she turned eighteen. She loved dancing and, on one of her
nights off, Kathleen walked into a ballroom where she would

meet her destiny. The glitter balls shone above and the young people eyed each other up as they stood on either side of the hall – but Kathleen's gaze was drawn to the dark, handsome young man in uniform who locked eyes with her as soon as she entered.

My father.

I love to think of that moment when they first set eyes on each other. Mum was a stunning woman with flaming red hair and a look of Katharine Hepburn about her. She had a lovely figure and always dressed well. I can imagine the moment when their eyes first met, and I know that, for her, it was like something out of a film. I'm sure it was the same for him too, but it's my mum's side of the tale which I took in, absorbed with every cell of my being, and learned by heart.

The ballroom was always busy. It was only ten years since the end of the Second World War and people were still in a bit of a post-war glow when it came to enjoying themselves. Getting out, being with other young people and dancing was a simple pleasure but one which meant a great deal after all that the country had been through. Women had become more independent during the war, being given opportunities to work – or, rather, being accepted as workers when there simply weren't the numbers of men to do everything previously seen as 'men's work'. Once they came back from the front, things changed to a certain extent in that men were still seen as the rightful holders of many positions, but women had experienced that sense of freedom and there had been a change in society. It was still very different to our current way of life, but there was a desperate need for fun, for happiness, and for simply grabbing on to life when everyone had seen how quickly such things could be taken away.

So, my parents met at a time when many young women were trying to break away from what was expected of them – and my mother was one of them. When she had been born, her future was no doubt seen as one of daughter, wife, and mother. She would be pigeonholed as someone who would marry then have children – the order was important – but something changed all of that. She fell in love.

I suppose every young woman back then hoped for that to happen to them. It wasn't so long since a whole generation had been used to their men being sent away, and far too few of them had come back. Romance was a great distraction from the losses that were still being felt, and young women of Mum's age seemed determined to make the most of life, of love, and of the future. I can't imagine that Granny Morag would have been sympathetic at any point. I'm sure she would have scoffed if Mum had told her any of this, and I know for a fact that she told her daughter to stop with her 'silly notions' and settle down with one of the lads who worked on the farm. Mum had no intention of doing any such thing, not once she met Dad.

My parents found each other at the dancing and they continued to meet there. Each weekend, after work, they would go to the Edinburgh ballrooms. She fell head over heels for my dad, a handsome Australian sailor named Brian. Nature took its course and she did what 'good' girls weren't supposed to do back then, although plenty of them did. She and Dad, nothing more than teenagers, found themselves in the middle of something they had never planned – a baby outside of wedlock.

I don't know the details of what went on when she told her mother, but I do know that she was told to stop working in Edinburgh and stay away from my dad. She defied the second of those rules and went into the city to meet him, and tell him that she had been told to have no further contact.

Dad's ship was returning to Australia and he promised that he would come back for her when he next got leave. They parted with many promises and a commitment to marry then raise their baby together.

Granny Morag was furious when Kathleen told her what had happened. She felt betrayed and also, knowing what I know of her now, angry that she had been defied. My mother was called a 'whore' and a disgrace. She was told that she had shamed the family and that she would never be allowed to forget the social embarrassment of having a bastard child. No matter how much she told her mother that my father loved her and would be back for her, she was laughed at and cursed. Granny Morag said that she pitied her own daughter's stupidity for believing a man and that she would never see him again.

She was right – but not for the reasons Mum believed.

Throughout the pregnancy and after my birth there was no word from Brian in Australia. Finally my grandmother relented and told Mum that if she handed over his details she would track him down and work out what should be done.

Mum told her his full name and rank – and two weeks later

Granny Morag handed her a letter from the Australian Navy that proved he had died.

Mum was devastated. With a newborn baby in her arms and a mother who was still calling her every name under the sun, she felt as if she had no hope. She had always thought Brian would come for her.

'You should be pleased,' Granny told her. 'He would never have come back for you or the bastard – now you can just pretend you were married and he was killed. There's no one to say otherwise.'

Granny Morag had it all worked out. With this story in place, she could have her daughter and grandchild at home, under her watchful eye. It was a story she repeated to all and sundry, but, given that we lived in such a small community where everyone knew the business of everyone else, it's unlikely that anyone believed it. Morag could, of course, have claimed that her eldest daughter had married in secret, in Edinburgh, without her knowledge, but big bellies and shotgun weddings to men who were never seen resulted in raised eyebrows back then. I doubt anyone fell for it, but it was important to Granny Morag that she tried to save face. Probably no one would have come right out and said to her that she was lying, she was far too intimidating for that, but there would have been gossip and there would have been other stories created that were far closer to the truth.

It didn't matter to Morag. She had decided which version of the tale she wanted, and when she made decisions like that no one dared insult her with the truth.

Chapter 2

Goodbye Mummy

I've been told that, when I was born, Granny Morag took me from my mother's arms and told her that there was no point in getting attached. She encouraged Kathleen to get back to work, bring in some money for the household, and leave the baby alone. There's a reason for everything and, when I was much older, I found out some of Morag's story, which I think goes some way towards explaining her attitude and coldness during this time.

When she was a young woman, Morag had been put in an asylum on the outskirts of Edinburgh, for reasons which seem staggering to us nowadays. When she was only sixteen, she got pregnant to a local builder from across the Firth of Forth. Unmarried and shamed, her father had her committed. Sadly, this was the outcome for too many young women in those days, but at least my granny got out and made a life for herself with her own family. Some women never escaped, some were put in the 'madhouse' when teenagers and died there decades later despite having done nothing but get pregnant.

During and after the First World War society changed

rapidly. People grabbed on to life, young women were no doubt having sexual relationships with less commitment than they otherwise would as everyone tried to hold on to normality and seize the day. That may have worked fine in families with the money or social abilities to hide 'mistakes' but for working-class girls there were strict rules. Having babies outside of marriage was considered to be a sin worthy of the gravest punishment. Committing such young women to lunatic asylums wasn't that unusual, and it's unlikely that the father of Morag's first baby even knew she was pregnant much less that she had been locked up. Although Granny Morag had her baby, very little was ever said. She was in the asylum for a couple of years and the baby given to her parents while she was in there. The little boy died. When she came out, the same thing happened. Again, she became pregnant to a man who didn't marry her and, again, the baby died some time after birth. I wondered about that when I first heard the story. It seemed too much of a coincidence for a young, unmarried woman with two bastard children to have both of them die in mystifying circumstances with no witnesses to, or record of, what happened. When Granny Morag did marry, she went on to have many children, all of whom thrived, which in itself was odd I felt, given her record for babies who mysteriously died.

With this horrific story as her own experience, I suppose it is no surprise that Morag was less than supportive of her daughter. Perhaps it could have gone either way; perhaps she could have thought of her own terrible past and vowed to make things easier for Kathleen. Or perhaps it was too much for her and she simply repeated the patterns of the past. Whatever her reasons – and I do genuinely believe that her actions were partly the result of what she had gone through herself – Mum always felt that she had to steal time with me.

I don't remember much of those early years with Mum. What I do recall is that she started to work again, going back to hotels in Edinburgh to earn as much as she could. By the time I was a toddler, our time together always took the same pattern. She began to talk of a 'new life' and, while she lay on the grass or played with me, would tell me stories of what was ahead.

'We're going to go to America,' she would whisper. 'It's lovely there, Sheena. We'll have a big house with a swimming pool. You'll have your own room and lots of toys. We'll have a whole new life – away from here, away from all of them.'

She was saving every penny she could, working all the hours of the day, for this dream. It meant that I saw very little of her, but the time we did spend together was magical. I adored my beautiful, loving mother and I know that she loved me to bits.

What I didn't know was that when she spoke of 'us' going to America she meant her. At least to begin with, the plan was that I would follow later, once she had established herself and had enough money to support both of us. She was a strong woman and very brave to make the decision to go, but I can't help but wish she hadn't. If she had stayed, she would have had the life of her mother, no doubt. She was an unmarried mother, with a bastard child, from a working-class family. She never did put out the story about her imaginary husband dying in action, and everyone around us probably knew the truth of the situation, despite

Granny Morag sticking to her fantasy of a secret wedding to a departed sailor who had died a hero. If Mum had remained in the farmlands south of Edinburgh, all she could have hoped for would have been that some man would be willing to take her and her child on. She would have had more children and adapted to a life of domestic drudgery and bitter gratitude for the man who had 'saved' her. It was not what she wanted.

She read magazines and went to the cinema. She saw America as the land of opportunity and felt that it might accept a young woman like her, a young woman with dreams who would work hard to provide for her baby girl. It could have worked, it might have worked, had it not been for her own mother, a woman so twisted about her own life and the choices she had not been allowed to make that she saw no harm in ruining the lives of others.

I don't actually remember the day Mum left, which seems terribly sad to me. All I know is that she was no longer there and I knew she was taking too long for it simply to be one of her work shifts keeping her from home. After a while, Granny Morag would drop little comments about how I was on my own now, about how I didn't have my mother to fight my battles, about how I was going to have to learn about life the hard way. She also started to make remarks whenever there were visitors, usually neighbours dropping in for a cup of tea and a gossip. There would be discussions about her kindness and what a wonderful woman she was to take me on. She would sigh a lot and say that she was just doing her duty, then look at me as if she had all the cares of the world on her shoulders.

In the absence of my mother, Granny Morag was the constant figure in my young life. She was a complicated woman, and she would become more so as I got older, but I also have some very warm memories of her. She could be very kind and would go out of her way to help people. There were a lot of tramps around when I was little, and they would often walk for miles looking for odd jobs or a bit of food to keep them going. Living as we did in the countryside, they would often pass by our cottage and, on many occasions, there would be a tap at the kitchen window. I'd look up to see a dirty, bearded face there and a man with desperation etched all over him.

Usually they'd ask the 'missus' for a 'wee cup of tea' but Granny would make a huge sandwich (a 'piece') with thick home-made jam on it, a real doorstop, a great big sweet metal mug of tea, and a friendly word. They'd never get inside – they had fleas and there was an unspoken rule that they had to stay outside – but would sit on the step with whatever she had provided. We always had milk, given that we could get that from the dairy part of the farm, but, for a treat, we'd sometimes get a drop of tinned Carnation milk in a cup of tea – and the tramps were always offered that too.

While they were drinking and eating, she'd make them a big pile of pieces to take away with them. The wrappers from plain bread were waxed paper which she always kept for this purpose. The tramp would go off with a pile of sandwiches and a full belly. To this day, I always keep that bread wrapping too as it reminds me of her – it's a happy memory and I have precious few of them to hold on to.

Sometimes they would be given fresh scones too, and everyone around knew just how kind Morag was to tramps. They all thought she was brilliant and, in that sense, she was. She did have a nice side, but it wasn't always there.

I remember snippets of my life at that stage, from when I was two until four years old. The world was changing quickly and, although I suppose we were somewhat isolated living on the farm, we could get into town reasonably quickly if the weather was fine, and because there were so many of Granny's older children (my aunts and uncles) out working, there was always a link to the outside world.

We had vans coming round for everything – there were two grocers, a butcher, the lemonade van. All of them brought their wares to us and all of the other farming families, because people had neither the time nor the personal transport in those days to make trips into town every time they needed something.

Granny Morag was, however, notorious for the times she did go out of the farm for anything. She never took a bag for the shopping, but simply slung a couple of old pillowcases over her shoulder and, no matter the weather, trekked for miles. She would walk through hail, sleet and snow if she had a mind to, fill the pillowcases with her purchases and trudge back again. No one in the family dared offer to help as they knew she would take that as an insult – but there was many a neighbour who got an earful from her if they stopped and offered her a lift home. Once she had set her mind to do something, God help anyone who got in her way. She was a legend in that village. As I got older, her hair became whiter and longer and she would be seen walking through snowdrifts with her pillowcases full of provisions, asking for and taking help from no one.

Not only was she seen as a witch, but we were seen as a tribe. Granny had, after all, given birth to ten children who had lived, and was on her second husband. I don't think people knew what to do with us. On one hand, we were shunned as there were so many of us and Granny was rumoured to have old powers, but, on the other hand, she was a stalwart of the community and Granddad was a kind old man who everyone liked.

She always had a pot of soup on the go, or stovies ready, and she could always find food to feed anyone who turned up on her doorstep. I think, deep down, she was kind-hearted but often didn't know how to show it. She was sometimes embarrassed to be seen as helpful or caring, and she would certainly do her best to put on a front of coldness, swearing like a trooper and never being the sort of woman who was warm or tactile with her children (apart from the ones she marked out as clear favourites). Her kindness was often seen through her actions, but those actions were directed more towards outsiders than family, and she certainly showed very little gentleness in her relationship with me as I got older.

I'm not a medical professional and Morag would never have given any psychiatrist the time of day (as I would later find to my own cost), but I suspect that she had some sort of personality disorder. She could change so quickly and so unpredictably, but it was also as if *both* personalities were just as real as each other. I never felt that she was pretending to be someone bad when she was angry, or that she was pretending to be nice when she showed sympathy for the fact that I missed Mum. Both sides were genuine; she just flipped between the two without warning.

From the time Mum left, when I was two, the nice side was, naturally, the one I held out hope for. When it was in play, Granny Morag would hug me and sing to me, she'd tell me stories and make me feel special, but those were rare moments. However, I learned to look out for her temper, for the way her personality would change in a flash, without provocation or warning, and with the usual result that I would be on the other end of a slap or a sharp tongue.

As I've said, she had a filthy mouth and I was used to being called a little bitch or bastard (or worse), but, then again, so was everyone else. She didn't save her cursing for me – she called everyone every name under the sun. I can't even remember the first time she hit me. I do think that it was after Mum left though. I can only imagine that Granny would have had a lot of explaining to do had my mother come back to a bruised or crying child. However, I also know that, by the time I was four, I was regularly slapped for minor misdemeanours, most of them unpredictably labelled as 'badness' by Granny Morag, even if they had been perfectly acceptable the day before. I would get hit for leaving a sweetie wrapper lying around, not tidying my toys away, being too loud, being too quiet, 'annoying' her, being too playful, wanting a nap, asking for something to eat, not finishing my dinner. There was no way of telling what would incur her wrath from one day to the next, so I did what so many children do in those circumstances – I stopped trying to predict what would upset Granny and cause her to hit me, and just got used to it being part of my life.

Despite all of that, her casual violence and her cruel words, I did love her. I did love my granny; but I wanted my mummy. By the time I was four, it was clear that the American dream was taking an awfully long time to happen, but I still hoped – I still hoped that Mummy would come.

Chapter 3

Everything has a beginning

It was always noisy and busy when I was little simply because I was part of a huge family – someone was always up to something. As I've said, Granny Morag was on her second husband and had ten children. Her first man had died of heart failure long before I was born, and her second, Big Kenny, was a lovely man but completely under her thumb. She'd had five children to each husband and it was almost as if there were two families. By the time I came along, the first five of Morag's kids were all working and away from home, while the next five were raised alongside me as if we were all brothers and sisters; they were slapped and shouted at just as much as I was, apart from her favourites. Granny Morag would go out to places such as bingo or shopping with one of her older daughters – usually her favoured girl from the first batch of children, Betty – as if they were friends rather than mother and child.

Granny and Granddad Kenny had separate bedrooms. This was entirely at her demand. She may have been physically small, but she was a strong, determined woman who ruled the roost and kept Kenny in his place at all times. He was such a gentle, happy soul that he never made any fuss, and Morag got to do whatever she wanted. So she had a bedroom of her own, which was full of solid, old-fashioned furniture that had probably been in the family for generations. When I got older and started to see other people buying modern wardrobes and beds from fancy new department stores, I was green with envy. Like so many people, I never realised just what we had – the things in Granny's bedroom alone would have had an antiques collector rubbing his hands with glee, whereas I would end up lusting after flat-pack furniture which would fall apart before the ink had set on the six-month guarantee!

Granny had some pretty things in her room, but she wasn't a fancy, frilly sort of woman, so they were few and far between, but her big double bed was piled high with pillows and eiderdowns, and was by far the softest and most comfortable of any in the house. Granddad had a smaller and very basic bedroom. There were two other bedrooms – one for the three boys and one for the two girls who were still at home. The boys were Robbie, Freddie and Jed, Jed being the youngest and the apple of Granny's eye. Jed had been in an accident when he was a toddler. I never did get the full story, but somehow he had got hold of a knife and done a lot of damage to his hand, with the result that one of his fingers had been amputated. Granny had always blamed herself for this and I believe this was why she was so attached to him. He was the centre of her universe and could do no wrong in her eyes. I don't know how much of that was to do with the accident, or to do with him being her last 'baby', but it was something that everyone knew and accepted. Jed was her world.

Morag was never shy at showing her favouritism. I shared a bedroom with her two daughters by Kenny, Nellie and Rose. Her attitude to them could not have been more different. Nellie was her favourite girl by far, and would always – like Jed – get away with anything, while she seemed to almost despise her youngest daughter, Rose, and would, in later years, make her life a misery. I always had a soft spot for Rose, and when I was snuggled in bed between the two teenagers would wrap my arms around her in the nights when I felt the loss of my own mother.

We didn't have much in the way of material things, but, living on a farm, we were never short of food. Just as I was jealous of those with fancy new furniture, I used to drool over fish fingers, or the new hamburgers which were appearing, completely oblivious to the fact that we lived on freshly churned creamy milk, huge steaks, and grouse! Granny was always cooking. There would be soup and bread being made all the time, and it seemed as if there was someone peeling potatoes at the sink on a permanent basis. In fact, that was the first chore I was taught, when I was so small that I had to be lifted onto a chair to even reach the sink.

When Mum left for America, I was bereft – but I was also very young. I didn't want her to go, but she had made me such wonderful promises, and I believed that she would return for me. I would be lying if I said that I spent every day in tears at the loss of her. There were always things to do on the farm, things to look at, things to play with. On top of this, I was so young when she went that I don't remember every specific moment of every day. I remember general things – she was there, then she wasn't –

but there was also continuity in my life. I was still living with Granny and Granddad and lots of my aunties and uncles, just as I always had. The only difference was that Mummy was no longer there.

Betty, one of Morag's first five children, had wed just a few months before Mum left. Her husband, Charlie, was from a huge family too. In fact, I never knew just how many Johnstones there were, but I started to spend a lot of time around them. Betty and Charlie were living with his widowed mother in a village a few miles from where we were.

The Johnstones were a big, ramshackle family and the matriarch at the centre of them all was a warm-hearted woman who, like my own Granny, always seemed to be cooking and baking. However, she did it with a better nature than Morag. Gladys usually had a smile on her face, and I never heard her swear, whereas Granny would put a docker to shame with her filthy mouth. After Mum left, I was often sent to the newly married Betty so that Granny could get a 'break' from me. I was about five years younger than her youngest child – Jed – and she was keen to tell everyone who would listen that I was wearing her out, that she was too old for all of this 'nonsense', and that Betty needed to take me now and again or she'd go mad. Actually, Morag couldn't have been that old – she was probably in her late forties when Mum left, which seems like nothing now. However, she certainly laid it on thick when telling anyone of the terrible burden of her deserted granddaughter and the drain it was on her.

I think the desertion which bothered her most was not that of my mother leaving me, but of my mother leaving *her*. When

Mum went to America, she was the first person to break away and I believe that sat very badly with the woman who was left in charge of me. For a little while she was fine. She was never a cuddly, emotionally demonstrative person, but she wasn't nasty or vindictive towards me at the start. That changed. Perhaps she thought Mum would return home with her tail between her legs, or that she would miss her; perhaps she thought her eldest child wouldn't be able to cope on the other side of the world, alone and without her huge family. When it became clear that Mum wasn't coming back in any hurry and it looked as if she was going to stay there for a year and make a life for us both, something changed in my granny. Looking back and remembering snippets of conversations, as well as things she said in later years, I also think that she went through the menopause at that time. Could that have changed her? Maybe. So much of her life had revolved around childbearing and child-rearing that it is entirely possible she found herself adrift. Unsure of her place in the world now that her fertility was at an end, she became a caricature of a bitter, emotionally repressed old woman who liked to stamp out joy wherever she found it, unless it was being experienced by her favourite children, Betty (now married to Charlie), Nellie and the golden boy, Jed.

I was not in that favoured group.

I was a daily, constant reminder to her of the child who had left. Mum's desertion seemed to gnaw away at her, who then took it out on the little girl who so desperately needed love and security. I would be sent to Betty's as often as possible, sometimes for weeks on end. I didn't like Betty very much, she always seemed to be in a bad mood and, like her mother, wasn't warm or cuddly, but I did like her mother-in-law, Gladys. There was someone else in that house who I really liked as well. Two of Gladys's sons still lived there, Eddie and Gerry. Neither of them worked. Eddie, like Jed, was his mother's favourite and totally indulged in everything he did. His younger brother, Gerry, was what we called back then 'simple'. I don't know what exactly was wrong with Gerry, or what form of learning difficulties he had, but he was the kindest, gentlest soul who ever walked the earth. He was a child in the body of a man really, and he was never happier than when he was around children. All Gerry wanted to do was play. If you had a ball – or, even better, a bat *and* a ball – he would play for hours. He wasn't like the other adults, who would 'shoo' you away or say they were too busy; Gerry was never too busy for fun and games. I absolutely adored him and never minded going to stay with Betty because Gerry was there.

To begin with I wasn't so sure about Eddie. It wasn't that I didn't like him, or that he did anything to make me actively *dis*-like him, it was just that he was quite morose at times. He didn't really do much, he just watched people. Most of all, he wasn't Gerry, and that was his biggest failing in my eyes.

When I was four, I feel I was with Betty (and, by extension, Gladys and her family) as much as I was with Granny Morag. When I got back to our cottage I'd ask if Mummy was there.

She never was.

And of course every time I heard a plane, I'd race out of the door, shouting, 'Mummy! Mummy!'

I could never predict what Granny's response would be.

Sometimes she'd say, 'That's a bloody sin, you poor wee soul, thinking she'll come back.' On very rare occasions she'd cuddle me as I cried, but she could be an old bugger too, and she'd be just as likely to tell me to stop my snivelling. 'Your mother's off having a grand time while I'm left to look after you, you wee bitch!' she'd shout. 'She's off making a new life for herself and I'm stuck here!'

I started to look forward to the occasions when I was sent to Betty – not because I liked Betty, but because the Johnstone house was such a good place to be. The first few times Granny took me on the bus, which went from village to village. It would stop at the fish-and-chip shop near to where Auntie Betty lived and she'd be waiting there to meet us. Everyone knew everyone in those days, and after a while Granny stopped taking me. She'd put me on the bus, and chat to the driver, telling him that Betty would meet me at the shop. He knew all of the family anyway. I was only four, but childhood was different back then and no one thought anything of packing a child off on its own. It was assumed to be safe. If a stranger had approached me, the driver would have done something, and I was being met at the other end by my auntie. What could go wrong?

Betty actually only met me on a couple of occasions. She was pregnant when she married Charlie, and by the time I was travelling alone she was too big and too tired to walk anywhere she could avoid. By the time baby Tracy was born nothing would get her to come for me, so she always sent Eddie, her brother-in-law.

Eddie would get me off the bus, often with Gerry at his side, and we'd head back to his mother's. To begin with I loved it there. I loved the new baby and another brother called Patrick who was stone deaf. He was so funny, and a lovely, nice man, just like Gerry but with a bit more about him. The house had four bedrooms and was always full, everyone had fun and there were people spilling out of every room. At weekends the men would go to the pub and come back drunk. I was usually still up, and I would love it when they started singing and having a laugh. There would be fights if someone stole someone else's song, but it was light-hearted. Half the time they didn't even know the words; it was like living in the middle of a Billy Connolly mono-logue! There were coats on the bed to keep the kids warm, and a constant stream of food and drink.

Gladys was very old-fashioned in her ways. She set the table with her best cloth and china every Saturday and Sunday. There were little tea plates and china cups with a rose pattern from her wedding service. She had a cake plate full of delicious things, and there was always a plate of plain bread with big crusts and brown bread too, set beside little jars of butter and jam. You chose the bread and topping you wanted – my favourite was banana with thick, sliced butter and sugar, or Nestlé milk, on white bread. It was probably a heart attack on a plate, but we knew no better back then. I always wanted the last slice, or the 'outsider' as it was called, and everyone was so nice, making sure I got it each time.

I felt safe and warm and happy there.

Gerry was always around to play with, which was the best thing of all, but Eddie had started wanting to play too. I didn't like that so much – he played differently, and it wasn't fun. He lifted me up a lot, always in front of other people, but he also touched me underneath my dresses.

I didn't like that.

I didn't like it at all.

However, I tried to put it out of my mind. I loved that house when it was full and noisy and busy and happy, so the times when Eddie touched me were, in some way, just something I had to put up with. I didn't know why he would want to touch me *there*. It was always where my knickers were and, sometimes, he would put his fingers inside my pants, which I couldn't understand at all.

I was only four. I had no idea that he was grooming me, that he was checking to see whether I would say anything to anyone while he did this in public. How could I know it was just the start of the monstrous things he would do to me, and how could I tell that he was being incredibly cunning by making others comment on how great he was with me, how patient and how playful?

There were other things about Eddie that made me uncomfortable. He cuddled me too much. This might seem an odd thing for a motherless child to complain about, but I didn't like his type of cuddles, I didn't like the way there was always saliva hanging out of his mouth, or how his hands wandered when he cuddled me. Eddie just touched me *too* much. It felt 'not nice'. I was very little and just had a sense of something not being right but I didn't have the words or concepts to explain it. On top of that, I didn't really like being too close to him because he smelled. He had brown teeth, stank of tobacco, and never seemed to wash.

Once, when I tried to wriggle away from him as his fingers went under my dress and into my knickers, I remember someone saying, 'Here, Eddie, maybe you should brush your teeth once in a while, then that bairn wouldn't be trying to get away!' He just laughed it off, but I did wonder why he was the only one who did that when we played. Why were his hands inside my knickers so much?

He would do play-fighting as well. He would pretend that he was wrestling me on the sofa and that it was a tremendous piece of fun, but he was the only one laughing as I tried to get away, and it always seemed to be purely so that he could touch me in places he shouldn't. I don't know how long this went on for, but I do know that it progressed to a point whereby he would be putting his fingers inside me on a regular basis, making sure that the play-fighting and piggybacks happened many times a day when I was staying with Betty.

I was torn between wanting to play – I was four years old; I always wanted to play – and hating the play which involved *that*. At first, I couldn't predict when Eddie would touch me. There would be times when he 'just' played, but, as time went on, I could predict it very well, because it happened every single time. He was seen by others in the family as being patient with me, as always having time to play horsey and pretend wrestling, and if there were times when I cried out there was no surprise to that. I was little and he would make up some excuse such as that I had fallen awkwardly or jarred myself or twisted a muscle. Even if I did say something about him touching me, I didn't have the words for it, so he would brush it off with a comment about 'tickling' or something like that. No one was paying attention anyway. They were all grateful that Eddie was entertaining Kathleen's abandoned child, and it was one thing less for them to do. For Betty in particular I had become a burden. Her mother offloaded me as much as possible and now that Betty had her own baby she was delighted that Eddie would step in and keep me quiet for a while.

I adored Gerry. When he was the one playing with me I knew it would be safe and I knew it would be innocent fun as he was just like a child himself. Eddie was a different kettle of fish. He was sly and cunning, he touched me in full view of everyone else and hid it behind the excuse of 'play'. He was very good at it – I know in retrospect that I was not the first child he had done these things to, and I know that in a harsh world where many people were struggling to get by he exploited his willingness to play and look after children to maximum effect. I just had no idea how far he would go.

Chapter 4

Jail

Betty and Charlie finally moved into a house of their own with baby Tracy. It was close to Gladys, so I still saw everyone when I went there and, to be honest, Betty always tried to offload me as often as she could, just as her mother did. Granny Morag would send me on the bus with bags of shopping for her daughter as well as a few coins so that I could buy a cake from the baker when I got there. Usually Eddie and Gerry met me from the bus but, one day, as the doors opened and the driver said 'goodbye' to me, I saw that it was only Eddie standing there.

He took the bags from me and started to walk off.

'Can I go for a cake, Eddie?' I asked excitedly.

'No,' he answered abruptly.

'I've got money! Granny gave me money!' I told him, as that seemed to me the only possible reason for refusing me the treat.

'I said no!' he snapped.

I didn't give up. I wanted my cake. I had money.

'Please?' I pleaded. 'Please, Eddie? Please can I buy a cake?'

'No – but you can shut the fuck up!' he snarled.

He put both shopping bags into one hand – they were light as I had to carry them off the bus anyway – and grabbed me with the other. I tried to pull my wrist away, but it was impossible given the difference in our strengths.

He dragged me up the street. Despite the fact that I was whimpering and protesting, no one took any notice. It wasn't that busy, but, even if it had been, there would have been no fuss made of a grown man with a moaning four-year-old. In those days people minded their own business. Children were the property of their parents and physical punishment was the norm. Children were regularly hit by parents and other family members, teachers were allowed to use the belt, and even neighbours or police officers would respond to naughtiness with a clip round the ear. There was very little awareness of any form of child abuse, there were no help lines or publicity campaigns, and a little girl complaining that she wanted a cake would not even have registered with anyone walking past.

So when Eddie pulled me into a public toilet there was no one looking out for me. There were two toilets, next door to each other, with separate entrance doors at the sides. The left-hand one, furthest from the street, was the male public toilet and it was in there that I was dragged.

At first, I suspected nothing.

Eddie muttered, 'I need the toilet,' and I thought nothing of being hauled in behind him. I thought nothing of the fact that he had looked inside first to see if there was anyone else there. I thought nothing of the fact that he had checked behind him and along the street, as he yanked my wrist and my body in there beside him.

I did say that I shouldn't go in because it was for men, but he silenced me.

'You'll have to,' he told me, 'it's not safe to leave you out here on your own, there's no one to watch you.'

'Can I get my cake when you're done?' I asked, still thinking that was the most important thing.

He stared at me. 'We'll see.'

When we went in, it smelled of cleaning fluids and urinal cakes.

'I need a pee,' Eddie said sharply, and put a penny in the door for a cubicle. There was no one at the urinals, no one else in there at all from what I could tell. He closed the door behind him and I heard him urinate. While I stood there thinking of my cake, he kicked the door open. He was sitting on the toilet but his trousers were pulled up. I didn't know what was going on.

'Come here,' he said.

'It's all right, Eddie,' I said, 'I don't need to go.'

'Come here anyway,' he commanded.

I hesitated but he reached out and pulled me in, closing the door behind us.

'Really, Eddie, I don't need. I'll tell you if I need the toilet,' I said again.

'Shut up,' he told me as he started to pull my pants down. I was a little cross at this point as I thought that he was ignoring me. He'd ignored my pleas for a cake, even though I had my own money, and now he didn't seem to believe me when I said that I didn't need the toilet.

I tried to pull my pants up, but he brought me closer to him and forced my hand onto something he had in his trousers. I had no idea what it was. There seemed to be something hard in there. I thought he had hidden something. I was clueless.

He made me touch whatever it was for what seemed to be a long time, and touched me too, then he stood up and pulled his own pants and trousers down.

'Sit here,' he said, putting me on his lap, sideways so that he could continue to make me touch him. The thing that I had felt through his trousers seemed to be attached to him. It was huge, horrifying, terrifying.

'Look what you've done,' he said, nodding towards the thing. It was hot and seemed to pulse; I didn't even know if it was part of him at that stage. 'Look at what you've done,' he repeated.

'I didn't do anything, Eddie,' I whispered.

'Oh, but you did,' he replied. 'That wasn't there before you started. That's all your fault.'

What is my fault, I wondered? What was it? Where had it come from, and had I really done something to make it happen? I honestly didn't know because I didn't know what it was in the first place.

'See if you don't sort this,' he said, 'I'll die.'

'No, Eddie, no!' I shouted, appalled.

'Aye, I will. I'll die. And you need to keep your voice down because if anyone finds out you've done this to me, you'll be in trouble. Do you know what happens to wee girls who do this to people?'

I shook my head.

'They go to jail. They go to jail if someone discovers that they made this happen, and they go to jail if they don't help out and the man dies. Do you want to go to jail, Sheena?' he asked.

'No, Eddie, no I don't!' It was the worst thing I could think of.

'Well, you'll have to help me then – you'll have to sort it. Will you do that?' he asked.

'I don't know how, Eddie,' I whimpered.

'Well, you better learn fucking fast,' he snapped. 'If you don't, you're not the only one who'll go to jail. Your granny will too. And Betty. And wee baby Tracy.'

I'm sure my eyes must have been the size of saucers by this point. I was crying as quietly as I could manage and shaking at the thought of being imprisoned and being responsible for everyone else being jailed too.

'They'll get your mammy as well, Sheena. They'll get her back from America and throw her in jail – but you'll never see her. She'll know it was your fault, but you'll never see her again.'

I believed him. I believed him completely. I knew about jail, and I knew about Carstairs high-security mental hospital, as Granny often spoke of men she knew who were being sent there for various things. I knew jail was real and I knew people were sent there. I thought that, if I had done a bad thing, it would happen to me too, and the horror of prison was worse than the horror of whatever I was going to have to do to 'help' Eddie.

As I sat there, on his lap, with my knickers at my feet and my bare bottom on his leg, he made me touch him. He put my hand on his penis and showed me what to do, moving my hand backwards and forwards as I got more and more upset. He started grunting and his words all ran into each other. He made me go faster and faster, keeping his hand on mine and pushing himself closer to me. When he finished, he pulled me closer and downwards. That's what I remember very clearly – that he ejaculated all over my neck and body. I had no idea what it was either; I had no idea what any of it was. The only thing I could think was that it was white blood and that I had hurt him even more, perhaps bursting the thing which was attached to him.

I burst out crying.

'I'm sorry, Eddie, I'm so sorry!' I apologised over and over again. I thought he might still die and I was terribly upset.

Finally, he seemed to recover a little. 'Aye, well, that was all your fault – don't you forget it. I think I'll be all right now, but if that happens again, if you do that to me again, you'll have to help me. If you don't, I'll die – and you'll go to jail. Do you understand?'

I did understand. I was bad and this was what I had to do to protect myself and my family. What I didn't understand was that he was preparing me; he was, in effect, telling me that it *was* going to happen again and that I would have to do all of this as often as he told me.

I was scared and I was crying.

'I don't want you to die,' I wailed. 'I love you, Eddie, I do, I want you to be fine and not die. Please don't die!'

It was true, I did love him. He was family and he was nice to me sometimes, and those times were what mattered in my eyes.

He was changing back to nice Eddie. 'Well, it's done for a while, but if that happens again,' he emphasised, 'you have to help me, Sheena. You have to. It was all your fault, but maybe we can keep everyone out of jail if we're careful and keep this to ourselves.'

I didn't know what I'd done, but I promised myself – and Eddie – that I would always help if I could.

'I hope it doesn't happen,' I whispered.

'But it might,' he replied, still preparing me for what he was planning.

'I'll help you, I will,' I said, the thought of the consequences looming large.

It was as if he could read my mind. 'Well, if it does, you'll have to. And you can't tell anyone. You know what happens to lassies like you – they go to jail.' It wasn't a question, it was a statement of fact. Through these words he was also telling me that this happened, it happened to others, it was common and I just hadn't known about it before.

Eddie put me on the floor and I pulled my pants up. I remember thinking *You shouldn't take your pants off in front of men.* I got that from my granny. She often said, 'Don't run around with no pants on in front of the laddies!' She'd fly after the girls with a wooden spoon if they came into a room in just their nightdresses if their brothers were there. 'What are you walking about like that for?' she'd yell. 'Making shame of yourselves!' When I thought of her saying things like that, I realised that I had done another bad thing in letting Eddie Johnstone take my knickers off. I had done so many bad things, so very many.

As all of this went through my head, he wiped me down. Whatever had come out of that thing of his – the white blood – was all over me, and he used scratchy, hard public toilet paper called Izal to try and clean it off. The paper was in little cardboard boxes and was completely non-absorbent. While Eddie made a poor attempt at cleaning me up I tried to work out what had happened but I didn't know the words for any of it.

'I don't want to make you bleed like that, Eddie,' I said.

'I won't die now, you sorted it,' he replied. 'I'm fine now.'

'I was bad though, Eddie, I was bad,' I continued, desperately trying to make sense of what had gone on.

'Aye, you were – but you sorted it and no one found out; that's what matters,' he said.

We walked out into the sunshine. It was a miracle that no one had come in, but maybe luck is always with men like Eddie. It certainly never seems to be with wee girls like me.

'Shall we go get that cake now?' he asked.

'Aye, Eddie!' I grinned, happily, delighted that he had forgiven me despite the terrible things I had done to him. 'That'd be lovely.'

We went to the baker's and he bought me a haystack cake. It was red and coconut-shaped like an upside-down haystack. The coconut was stuck to pink jam and there was sponge inside. I hate those cakes now. He knew it was the type of cake I loved then and, as I ate it walking up the road, relief flooded over me that everything had ended so well.

If I could go back in time, I would kill him.

I never gave what had just happened another thought that time; I was simply looking forward to seeing everyone else. Eddie took me back to his mother's house, and Betty was waiting there with the baby. I do remember that Gerry looked at us strangely when we went in, and someone, maybe him, made a comment about us taking a while. Eddie laughed it off, and then Gerry expressed surprise that I had my cake already, that I hadn't waited until he had taken me for it.

However, as the years pass, I don't know how much I'm reading into all of that. Gerry wasn't smart, he could barely function on his own, so I have no idea whether he did suspect anything at that stage, but I do know that he was very good at recognising patterns, because he liked things to stay the same and to be able to predict what was going to happen based on the habits of everyone in the family. Perhaps he did sense that something was wrong, that something different had happened, but, to be honest, even if he had jumped up on a table and shouted *Eddie has just abused Sheena!* at the top of his voice no one would have cared. Anything he said against his brother would have been dismissed – he was seen as the daft one after all.

Over that weekend, Eddie was very nice to me in front of the others. He was playful – without there being any inappropriate touching – and he cuddled me a great deal. He sang songs to me, even though he wasn't a good singer, and he made a great show of being attentive and caring. I went between Betty's new house and the home where Gladys stayed with the remainder of her family. I felt safe. How awful – despite what had happened, I felt safe. It was almost as if the terrible experience I had gone through in the public toilets with Eddie had given me some protection from him. As the weekend passed, I managed to forget the terror of the thing he had down his trousers, the white blood, the threats of punishment and what would happen if I ever made that thing hard again. I was fed and cleaned, I was kept warm and was part of a big, loud family with their usual weekends of drinking and laughing. At the heart of it all was Gerry: good, kind Gerry. He watched over me a lot that time. He would stroke my hair and cuddle me as I dozed before bedtime. He told me that he loved me – but never once did he say he would look after me. I guess he knew that he couldn't. I guess even poor, simple Gerry knew some things – and one of those things was that his brother was in charge.

Eddie. Sharp-featured, fast-moving Eddie. He had them all wrapped round his little finger. His mother thought the sun shone out of his backside. Most of his brothers and sisters (although not all, as I would increasingly find out) thought he was a great guy. Betty trusted him with the child she was supposed to be in charge of.

And me? Even I had said I loved him mere moments after he had abused me. As the pain and fear of what had happened started to fade I prepared to go back to Granny Morag. Betty took me to the Johnstone house to say goodbye for that visit, and they all said they'd see me soon. Eddie bent down to pick me up, wrapped me tightly in his arms and said he'd miss me. 'And remember, Sheena,' he whispered into my ear, unknown to the others as they looked on, 'remember the jail – and remember your mammy locked up for ever if you don't help me. You remember that, Sheena. You remember it.'

Chapter 5

Rituals

The Johnstone family had their rituals. Every Saturday, Gladys would go shopping with her daughter Celia. They would spend the day getting bits and pieces, treating themselves to lunch, then they would arrive back home at teatime, ready to watch the wrestling on TV with the rest of the family. This was a tradition for everyone – and you could set your watch by the time Gladys and Celia left as well as by the time they got back.

Betty and Charlie lived in their new house, with baby Tracy, just around the corner. They were in and out of each other's places all day long, as everyone tended to be in those days, but when Gladys was shopping with Celia, Betty had no reason to go round there. Betty's main aim in life was to get out of doing things and her Saturday morning tradition was to send me to the Johnstones with a betting slip for her husband, Charlie. She would give me the money and a slip (Charlie couldn't put it on himself as he worked on Saturdays) and I was expected to pass it all straight to Eddie, who was seen as the reliable brother. While Eddie went to the bookies, Gerry would be told to take me to the swing park. I loved it when that happened. Gerry wasn't like the other grown-ups; he'd play for hours, never get bored or tell you to hurry up, and he seemed to enjoy himself too. On the first trip back to them all after Eddie had abused me in the public toilets, Betty sent me, as usual, to give him the betting slip for Charlie.

'You've to put this on,' I said when I got in, skipping over to Gerry. 'Are we going to the swings, Gerry?' I asked.

Just as he nodded, his brother interrupted.

'No – not today,' he said.

'Aye,' said Gerry, 'aye, Eddie – I take wee Sheena to the swings.'

'Not today,' his big brother repeated.

Gerry looked confused. 'I take wee Sheena to the swings,' he said, nodding again to confirm to himself that this always happened.

'I said not today,' Eddie told him.

'But Eddie . . .' began Gerry, only to be cut off.

'Here, Gerry, do you want some coins for the tossing?' Eddie asked.

He needed to say nothing else. Gerry's eyes lit up as if it was Christmas. All the old men in the village used to gather in a field and toss coins. It seemed like a very dull game to me, but Gerry adored it. Basically they just threw coins to see which landed furthest, or there would be a main coin and each player would try to get his coin closest to it. It was very simple and repetitive, which is why Gerry liked it. It was his favourite thing in the world and he was always looking for spare coins so he could take part.

'I'll look after Sheena – you take Charlie's bet to the bookies, and I'll give you some coins for the tossing for your trouble,' Eddie told him, smiling.

'Really?' asked Gerry, unable to believe his luck.

'Aye, really!' he replied. 'You'd be doing me a favour – I'll give you two shillings; turn them into pennies at the bookies when you put Charlie's line on.'*

'Two shillings?' repeated Gerry. 'Just for me?'

He would be trying – and failing – to calculate just how many big, brown pennies he would get for that and how long he would be able to stay at the tossing for.

Eddie smiled indulgently and gave him the money. Gerry took it and headed off to the betting shop without a backwards glance at me. I knew I would be alone with Eddie for a few hours at least as Gerry lost track of time when he was at the tossing.

I also knew that there would be no one else in the house that day. People were working, Betty wouldn't risk coming round, not when she'd managed to get rid of me, Gladys and Celia wouldn't be back until the wrestling started. No, until Gerry returned – which would only be when everyone else left the tossing – it would just be me and Eddie.

I think that was the day when I realised what the new ritual was.

Gerry was barely out of the door when *it* happened again.

'Look, Sheena,' said Eddie. 'Look what's happened.'

And that was it. That was the pattern. It was as if he had broken through after the abuse in the public toilets and now it was

* Scottish vernacular for putting a bet on

just something he did to me. The thing – which I soon realised was indeed attached to Eddie and was a part of his body – had got big and hard again. Only I could help as I had made it happen in the first place. He showed me what to do with my hands and the white blood came out again. All the time he kept whispering to me the threats about jail and about never seeing my mummy again. The only time he stopped saying that was when he was making his strange grunting and panting just before the blood appeared.

When it was all over, he did just as he had last time – he warned me that I would always have to 'help' him, then he acted as if nothing untoward had gone on at all. In fact, he made me some toast and sat at the table looking at the racing pages. After some time we walked down to meet Gerry at the tossing. The normality of it all was what threw me and, I guess, it was meant to throw me. From Eddie's perspective, I can only assume that if he made me believe three things – it was my fault, I had a duty to 'fix it', and it was normal – then he was reducing the chance of me saying anything to anyone. The fear of jail was what really kept me quiet.

Every visit to Betty held the same pattern. I would sometimes go there at weekends, sometimes during the week as I wasn't at school yet. During the week Eddie would take his chances where he could and he also returned to the public toilets to abuse me, but it was on Saturdays, when Gladys was out and Gerry was going to the bookies with Charlie's bet and then to the tossing, that he could take his time. Eddie was devious and he was wicked – Gerry was none of that, but in his own way he was helping Eddie because if he had been there I don't think it would have happened so often or so brutally.

When I was back home, with Granny Morag, the terror of my badness resulting in Mummy being brought back from America to be thrown in jail haunted me. I wanted nothing more than for her to come home, to save me and to take me away to the land and life she had promised, but I didn't want to risk her being taken by the police straight to Carstairs because she had such an evil, naughty child.

I was being told that I was bad pretty much all of the time. Granny ranted and raved about the way in which her daughter had deserted me to go off and 'enjoy herself' but she always made sure that she threw in a few choice remarks about how she'd have run a bloody mile from me if she could. Every so often she'd change that and say that it was a damn shame that I had been thrown aside, but the insults were by far the common theme of her speeches. As I said, the neighbours and rest of the family all thought she was wonderful to take me on, but they didn't see the reality of it.

I continued to hold out a small sliver of hope that Mummy would come back to me. Every passing plane held promise, every roar of an overhead engine made me run outside to see if this was the day she would jump from the aircraft and hold me close before we left for America. When I was four and a half something changed. I had no idea how significant it was, but the fact that Granny Morag officially fostered me meant that the likelihood of Mummy coming back and rescuing me became even less.

From the story I pieced together as an adult, she told my mum it was necessary to get the documentation in place to give me a sense of security; but from what many family members have told me it was really down to a combination of money and revenge. The social work department paid my granny to foster me, even though she was family. The reason was because she said I had been deserted by my birth mother. Two of Morag's adult children co-signed the documents and that was all it took.

Granny never tried to make me call her 'Mummy' – there were boundaries in that sense – but she certainly took that place once the documents were signed. I've been told that she gloated over her new 'ownership' of me and informed everyone that Kathleen had now been put well and truly in her place; her only child had been signed away.

As a result of the fostering we were visited by social workers every so often, once a month I think. I was never allowed to be on my own with them; Granny was always there. She would put on a front with them, never swear, and make sure that she presented herself as the kindly granny who had taken on a deserted grand-daughter. She would give the social worker (usually a man) a Camp coffee as she thought that was really posh. I remember staring at the bottle with an Indian and a kilted soldier on the label, listening to the lies she was spinning about my mother. The social worker would always speak to Granny, not to me, and as I stood there, washed and in my best clothes, I suspect I was seen as a very lucky little girl to be taken in by such a wonderful woman.

Granny Morag would say that my mother was flighty, that she had always wanted rid of me, that she only thought of herself. She would say that it cost a fortune to bring me up and that she got nothing from my mother, that I ate her out of house and home, that I was always asking for fancy clothes that she worked her fingers to the bone to provide – and it was all lies. The pretty clothes I had came in parcels from my mummy in America. She sent money too, and I knew this because I went with Granny Morag to the bank so she could change the dollars into pounds. More than anything I hated that word *deserted*. I was not deserted. Mummy had left to make a new life for us. She *was* coming back and if it was taking a little longer than I had expected, well, I could cope with that because at least while she was in America she was safe from being thrown in jail as a result of my badness. I'd save Mummy – and then when she did come back, she'd save me.

Something changed in Morag once she fostered me. While she was Granny, she was fine, bearable, even nice sometimes; but once she became my mother, on paper, the cruelty and violence were what I associated with her on a daily basis. She wasn't some-one I could confide in, but, even if I had felt that I could, Eddie had me well warned. If I told anyone, it would be evidence of my badness and we'd all end up in jail. He'd die if I didn't help him with the bad thing, and I would be responsible for the collapse of two entire families. I was abused so much by him; it was every time I went there. I couldn't make sense of things but I knew that it was all my fault. On top of that, when Eddie said that this was what happened, I got a sense that it was part of a bigger picture, that it happened with other bad little girls, and that they had to do these things to make matters right as well.

One day, when he was looking after me and Betty was at her

own house with Tracy, he took me into the kitchen. No one else was around – it was the weekend and Gladys was off shopping with her daughter, while Gerry had been paid off with some coins for the tossing.

'Come on,' he said, 'I need a cup of tea. You can help me.'

I always had hope in my heart when it was like this. He could be nice to me, although it was usually after the abuse had happened. Something normal like making tea gave me a focus; I was only four, and had some vague notion that I could keep him busy doing that for hours until someone came back.

Eddie lifted me up onto a worktop next to the sink, so that I would be at the same level as him while he filled the kettle. I watched him as he pottered around, then he came back to where I was. He started touching my legs, running his hands up them from the ankles over my knees and higher.

I squirmed about on the worktop, but he kept doing it, pushing my dress further and further up.

'You've got nice wee drawers on there, haven't you?' he said, smiling as he looked at my knickers.

I was looking lovely that day. I had a whole new outfit on that had been sent from America. Mum had made friends with a couple who couldn't have children of their own and they had started to send me things too; I wasn't sure if this was a gift from them or Mum as I had so many outfits coming to me through the post on a regular basis. It made a mockery of Granny's claims that I was costing her a fortune. My dress, cardigan, socks and pants were all matching and I had been so proud of them when I put them on that day.

'I'm a bit worried,' said Eddie. 'We need to get the lunch ready and I don't want you getting dirty in your fancy get-up.'

I squirmed some more as he continued to touch me.

'We'll have to take those pants off as we're going to be peeling tatties and you might get in a mess.'

I had no idea how to get away – of course, there was no way I could have, but I still felt that there was something I should be trying to do to escape from the clutches of this horrible man. He slid my pants down my legs awkwardly as I sat on the worktop. Leering at me, he started to rub my legs with the knife he held for peeling the potatoes. He was moving it up and down my legs, not enough to make them bleed, but enough to leave red marks.

'That's sore, Eddie,' I said, trying to pull away. 'That's sore.'

I tried to pull away, but he grabbed me, saying, 'That bad thing's happening again, Sheena.'

'No, Eddie!' I shouted. 'I didn't do anything! Honest, I didn't!'

'The bad thing's happening, and you'll need to sort it,' he emphasised, his eyes darkening as I started to cry.

'I don't want to,' I said. I suddenly thought that I had a trump card. 'I don't want to, Eddie, because it might start to bleed again.'

He smiled.

'That's fine – that's you fixing it,' he told me. 'That's you being good – if you don't do it ... well, that's when the police might have to come and see you.'

I thought about this for a moment.

'But, Eddie,' I began, 'it must hurt. It must hurt when it bleeds the white stuff ...'

'Listen to me,' he snapped. 'You have to do it because it's your fault. If you don't, it'll swell up even more and then it'll burst. *Then* I'll die and it'll be your fault, your fault, your fault! You'll go to jail, Sheena, you will, and so will everyone else.'

I started crying even more at that point.

I didn't want to do it, I hated the idea of touching that thing.

I was shaking my head as he rubbed the knife up and down my legs, but I was also trying to pull my hand away from his. Perhaps Eddie sensed some defiance in me that day, because it was the first time that he thought of another way to terrify me. Under the sink there was an area with pots and pans and cleaning products. It was a horrible place as there were spiders and lots of other creepy-crawlies.

Eddie opened it and told me to get in. 'Crawl in,' he demanded.

It was a tiny space and I didn't want to go into it. I shook my head even more, but he grabbed me off the worktop and shoved me in. I was so little that it didn't take much effort.

He closed the door behind me. I could feel cobwebs and knew that there were all sorts of beasties in there. It smelled of damp and I started to think there might be mice – or even rats – as well. My imagination was running wild and I'm sure he would have known that.

'If you don't sort it, you'll need to stay in there all day!' he shouted.

I could hear him walking about and then heard something bang against the door. When I tried to push, I realised that he had wedged me in. I started to scream.

'I'll fix it, Eddie!' I bellowed. 'I'll fix the bad thing. I'll sort it.'

'Promise?' he asked, just outside the door which I was pounding upon.

'Yes. Yes, I promise. Just let me out, please, please, please!'

He let me out and pushed me towards the living room.

'Get through there and stop your fucking whining,' he snarled. 'This is all your fault anyway. What have you got to moan about?'

Whimpering, I walked to where I was directed.

'Get on that settee,' he told me.

I knew that he was cross, but I was willing to put up with that as long as he left me alone.

'I'm sorry, Eddie,' I began. 'I'll be good. I'll go to sleep. I won't bother you.'

One of the last things I remember from that time is his laugh.

He pushed me on my back and shoved my legs open. I had no idea why he was doing this. I still had no idea when he took his trousers and pants off and got on top of me. The pain shot through me and I thought that bones would break.

I passed out very quickly that day.

When I woke up, there was white blood all over me and I was aching. My private parts, the bits that no one was supposed to see or touch, were so sore and there was blood on me.

As an adult, one of the things that shocks me is how quickly it all escalated. He'd gone from touching me while we 'played' to this in a very short space of time, and he seemed to act in a way that suggested he had no fear of being caught by anyone.

When I came to, and saw my red blood and his white blood,

when I felt the pain and thought something had been broken, I saw him sitting beside me on the sofa, watching me.

'That was your fault,' he said, quietly but firmly. 'You do know that, right? It was your fault.'

I couldn't answer him. I couldn't find the strength to speak.

'Now listen to me – that, *that*, was the right way to do it, to fix things. It should have happened that way before, but I had to make do in the toilets. It wasn't my fault that you made it happen then, and there was nowhere to lie down. You know the right way now – make sure you remember that. And remember this too – the jail's always open for a bad lassie like you. Always open. Always waiting for you. I just need to say the word – never forget that.'

I tried to sit up, but the pain was intolerable. I don't know if he actually did fully rape me that day, but he certainly penetrated me to some extent. I would think that I was so small that he hadn't managed completely, but it was the start and he would certainly manage before long. My fear was that Eddie would try again and I prayed for someone to come in and prevent me being alone with him. For the first time, my prayers were answered and I heard Gerry open the front door. When he walked in I was on the sofa with my dress up around my waist, no knickers on, covered in blood and semen. Eddie was sitting beside me. There could be no doubting what had just gone on.

Gerry looked at me with a sadness I can remember to this day.

He walked over to me in silence, picked me up and took me to the bathroom.

This gentlest of simple men stood me in the bath and, as I

shook with fear, shock and pain, he sponged me down with warm water.

He cuddled me tightly and started talking, chanting the same words over and over again, comforting himself as much as me.

'You're all right, wee Sheena, you're all right, darling. Gerry no' hurt you, Gerry loves you, Gerry no' hurt you, Gerry no' hurt you.'

He was crying the whole time. He washed and dried me so tenderly, put my clothes back on and took me back to the living room. It wasn't the last time he would have to do all of that. I think he was used to cleaning up after Eddie and I think he had cleaned up after plenty of other children.

Eddie was in the kitchen, peeling those blasted potatoes. Gerry sat beside me after he'd put the television on. He busied himself, putting more coal on the fire, poking it up, but always coming back to me and stroking my hair.

After a little while Eddie came through with a tray for me. There was a cup of tea, some toast and a banana.

'Here,' he said, as if we were conspirators, 'I've got a wee treat for you.'

He pulled a chocolate biscuit out of his pocket. A Skippy.

'There you go – and d'you know what?' he asked, winking. 'We'll take you to the swings later. You'll like that, won't you? D'you want to go on the big slide? I'll stand at the bottom and Gerry'll take you up. Aye, you're just wee, but as long as you don't tell Betty, we'll be fine, eh?'

Gerry was quiet and subdued. He didn't say a word.

And me? A chocolate biscuit and a go on the big girl's slide. That was my reward.

Chapter 6

Sharing the pain

I spent that day with Eddie and Gerry. I got my afternoon at the play park as if nothing had happened. I suppose Gerry just tried to put it out of his mind, but he was quieter than usual and he did give me a lot of cuddles as if silently reassuring me. Eddie was chatty. He pushed me on the swings, helped me up the slide as he had promised – but throughout it all I was in agony. Every part of me seemed to ache. By the time Betty and the rest of the family appeared for dinner and to watch the wrestling with Gladys I could barely move.

Charlie stayed at his mother's house later than his wife, and I walked back to Betty's house with her and Tracy in the pram. Walking was excruciating and I just wanted to lie down. When we got in, Betty couldn't be bothered with me and said I should get ready for bed, even though it was barely seven o'clock.

As I lay there, I hoped that the pain would go, but it was all over and I felt as if I was on fire when I went to the toilet. I did try to sleep but it was impossible.

'Betty!' I called. 'Betty! I'm sore!'

I didn't think about it before I shouted. I didn't think about what Eddie had threatened me with, the things he had said about jail and never seeing my mummy again; I just responded naturally as a child of that age would. I was sore and I wanted something – someone – to make it better.

'Go to sleep!' she shouted back.

This went on for a while, with both of us calling the same things to each other, then I finally gave up and tottered through to her.

'My front bum's sore,' I told Betty.

She rolled her eyes and sighed.

'What have you done? Did you hurt it on the slide?' she asked.

'No,' I replied. 'Eddie did a bad thing.'

'What?' she hissed.

'Eddie did something to my wee bum,' I told her. This was what I called it – at four and a half, I had a wee bum and a big bum, or a front bum and a back bum.

'What? What did he do?'

I didn't really know, so I tried to explain it as best I could.

'He's got a thing,' I began, 'and it's a bad thing and it's my fault and I'll go to jail. But I'm sore, Betty.' I took my pants off as I stood there. They were covered in blood. 'I fixed his bad thing, Betty, but then Eddie hurt me with it – his thing hurt me and I'm sore and I'm bleeding.'

Eddie Johnstone has a lot to answer for in my life but, by God, so does Betty. Faced with a bleeding four-year-old who was telling her about abuse in the only words she could find, her response was appalling.

'You shut your mouth,' she said calmly, holding on to me with both of her hands. 'You shut your mouth. There's nothing wrong with you. Do you understand? There's nothing wrong with you.'

'But there is, Betty,' I said bravely. 'I'm sore.'

'Then you hurt yourself on the slide – right? Don't go on it again; you've been warned.'

With that, she shoved me away and I went back to my bed, aching and confused. After that, Betty told everyone that I made up stories. I was a liar. I couldn't be trusted or believed. She was covering for him too. Eddie was surrounded by people who let him carry on with what he was doing. And carry on was exactly what he did. He tried to penetrate me on every visit after that and, of course, one day he managed. I don't know when it was (although I do know I was still four), because it was gradual. It was as if he was chipping away at me every weekend I was there.

There were other relatives to visit, but those trips were much rarer. I had one uncle and auntie who lived near to Glasgow. They had a house close to a canal, and my uncle told me once that I needed to be careful because if I fell in I'd end up in Australia. So, I jumped! Australia seemed very far away from Eddie, which was what I wanted, and I had some notion that it was close to America so I might find my mum if I went that way.

The horror was so frequent that much of it became one terrible memory, but there was one day just before I started school that I'll never forget.

I was in Eddie's mum's house but I had been doing all I could to stay away from him. One of the biggest dilemmas for me was that I loved Gerry so much. He was such a lovely man, a real gentle soul who always had time for me. Of course, there is no doubt that he had what would now be called learning difficulties, but back then everyone just said that he was 'simple'. Actually, he was. It wasn't an insult from what I could see; he was a simple person with simple needs and a straightforward approach to life in which he never harmed anyone. I felt that he had watched me a lot since the time he had come in and seen me on the sofa after Eddie had tried to rape me – but there was nothing he could do.

He was the complete opposite to his brother, who I was coming to see as the Devil on Earth. I had been in the house all morning, and spent all of that time either with Gerry or just hanging around him trying to feel safe. However, Eddie had called him through to the living room and I was left alone in the kitchen. I waited for a few minutes; then decided to find Gerry. I had brought a new bat and ball with me that day and wanted him to play with me. He was always so patient and never said 'no'. I left the kitchen, picked up the toy from the hall and walked towards the living room where I knew both men were.

I could hear words coming from behind the door and I could also hear sounds that I couldn't understand. It all seemed quite muffled, and I was too little to make sense of everything in my world anyway. Something stopped me from pushing the door open further and going inside. I just knew that something wasn't right.

I listened for a while; standing there with my bat and ball in my hands I could hear grunting and groaning. Above it all, I could also hear Gerry saying, 'Don't do this, Eddie, don't do this.'

I couldn't hear Eddie's response to him. I was torn. Gerry was obviously upset and I loved him dearly, but I was terrified of Eddie. This man who had hurt me so much was obviously doing something bad to his brother, something I had no words for and which I couldn't really understand, but I knew fear and I could hear it in Gerry's voice.

Suddenly, something clicked.

The noise I could hear – it was the noise Eddie made when he was doing bad things to me. Gerry was crying and he kept saying, 'No, no, Eddie, please stop, don't do this, Eddie, don't do it.'

Thinking about it now, as an adult, and knowing what Eddie was like, what he liked to do, I believe that he must have been sodomising him. Eddie just didn't care who he abused. If you were there, you were fair game.

I was only tiny and I can't remember the rest of what happened. I must have slinked away, too scared of what might happen to me if I opened the door. Memories of then don't come packaged in neat little boxes. I can't open up one labelled 'Sheena, aged four years, six months' and get all of the details as clearly as if my life had been scripted. It comes in snatches. I remember bits of days, and don't always know how things ended, or even started. Part of the reason for this is that there was a lot of normality. I could be abused in the morning and then get my lunch as if nothing had happened; and, of course, nothing *had* happened in the eyes of others. So, that day, I probably just went back to the kitchen until it had finished.

It would have affected me though. Gerry was such a nice man.

He didn't want anyone to be hurt. He is one of the constants when I think about my childhood. I loved him dearly and I know that he loved me. Sometimes I wonder what my life would have been like if Gerry had been able to stand up for me – but, then again, if he had been free of his own difficulties perhaps Eddie would have been different in the first place anyway. As it was, I always enjoyed being with Gerry. He would play with me, laugh and joke, and just generally be there as an innocent adult in my world.

Before I went to school my feelings for Gerry were unchanged. He was a nice man, he didn't want anyone hurt and you could leave him alone with any child. Gerry got very upset if anyone seemed to be in pain, whether it was emotional or physical. He did the best he could with what faculties he had but he was severely disabled, by far the most disabled in a family riddled with problems. He was slack-jawed and would stand in the street shouting at cars for hours on end. People would say there was nothing in there; the lights were on but there was no one at home. If you had a bat and ball Gerry would play for hours. He'd stay at the swings for hours if you wanted, or go to the burn with a fishing net and a jar for minnows, or to the roundabouts, no matter the weather or the time.

How did Eddie keep him quiet, I wonder? Why did Gerry never say anything given that he didn't have the sense to keep a secret usually? Money for the tossing and fear, I think. Eddie probably had him well threatened because Eddie ruled the roost. His sisters were under his sway too and I would find out why when I was older.

He was the blue-eyed boy who could do no wrong in the mind of Gladys – but he was an evil, twisted bastard of a man. He did little jobs for his mum, gardening and suchlike, but it was all a front really. Gerry did it and Eddie got the glory. Eddie would potter about making the flowers look pretty but Gerry did the back-breaking stuff and Gladys would crow about her big, strong boy who smirked at how he managed to get everyone to think he was marvellous at the expense of Gerry's labour.

He was a skilful manipulator.

He was evil.

I think it was Gerry who really made me think about right and wrong. Although he had his troubles, he never touched me inappropriately; he only ever loved me in an innocent way. If a man like that knew never to hurt a child, then there was no excuse for Eddie to do what he did.

The Johnstones were a strange family. They didn't really have any friends outside their own relations. Granny Gladys went to kirk, but the others didn't, and Eddie never had any girlfriends. Gladys could never understand that. She thought he was handsome and wonderful; she thought they should all be queuing up for him, but there must have been suspicions, there must have been talk, because I never saw any lassie near him and, by God, some of them were desperate in those days.

When I was wee they seemed like 'The Broons', the cartoon family from our Sunday newspaper who lived together as one big daft rabble. It felt that way for a while when we were all sat at the table and everyone was nice and friendly, but I soon saw the other side.

Terrible things must have happened – they had dark secrets and they seemed to think that they should carry it on; that there was no shame in what was happening, no perversion or wrongness. Back then, there was no education about abuse, nothing at all, but I do wonder how they came to terms with it once television programmes started looking at the issue and they saw it was wrong and something to be condemned.

Of course, the abuse from Eddie never leaves me, but my overwhelming recollection of him – the thing which pops into my head whenever I have a memory of him in those days – is the smell of him. He was absolutely disgusting. Whenever he came near me, I wanted to retch. He never seemed clean; I was never aware of his personal odour getting less awful, so I wonder if he ever washed at all. He was a filthy man on every level.

One Saturday night, I was staying over at Betty's again. There was a party going on – they liked parties – and the house was full of people. I often had tummy upsets when I was there, which is unsurprising given that my body would be reacting to what I was expecting to happen and, on this night, I was badly constipated.

I was in a lot of pain, and went through to the bathroom on my own. I could hear all of the grown-ups, and a few other children, in the living room as I sat there by myself. My stomach was getting more and more sore, so I called on my auntie.

'Auntie Betty!' I shouted, trying to make myself heard above the noise of the music and laughter. 'Auntie Betty! I can't do the toilet properly! It really hurts!'

There was no reply, so I tried again. The pain in my tummy

was excruciating and I just wanted someone there with me, to tell me it would pass and I'd be fine. 'Auntie Betty!' I called again, 'please come through! My tummy really hurts!'

I heard her voice on the other side of the door.

'Will you shut up? Everyone can hear you. Do you think we all want to know you can't do the toilet? Now, be quiet, I'm feeding the baby.' I heard her footsteps fade and called out, 'But it's so sore, I think I'm going to burst!'

'Oh, for fuck's sake!' she snapped, exasperated. 'I've told you, I'm feeding the baby. I'll send someone else through to stop you whingeing.'

She sent Eddie.

As I sat there, desperately trying to go to the toilet and to stop myself from crying with the pain, he walked in.

'All right, wee Sheena?' he said.

My stomach clenched even more.

'I'm fine,' I lied.

'That's not what I heard. You been bothering your Auntie Betty?'

I shook my head.

'I'm fine. Really. I'm fine now. You can go.'

He smiled. I could see his horrible brown teeth close up as he came even closer to me and pushed his face towards mine.

'You sure? You sure you're fine now?'

I nodded. I just wanted him to go. I didn't want to be in the same room as him, and I certainly didn't want us to be alone together.

'Good,' he said, walking away from me. 'I'm glad you're feeling better.'

Of course, I wasn't. My tummy felt even worse now that he was here, but I'd say anything to make him leave. I'd sit in silence a mile away from the toilet all night if I had to.

I closed my eyes and thanked God that I had escaped from him this time. But I hadn't; I'd counted my blessings too soon, because he didn't leave the bathroom after all. When he got to the door, instead of walking out, he turned round, leered at me, gave a horrible sort of grin, and locked it.

'I'm glad you're feeling better, wee Sheena,' he smirked, 'because I've got something I need you to help me out with.'

With that, he unzipped his filthy trousers and put his hand inside. He pulled his penis out and started to play with himself. Eddie walked towards me, masturbating. I was still sitting on the toilet, and my face was level with it.

He was shoving himself in the direction of my mouth, but I couldn't quite believe what he wanted me to do.

I shook my head. 'No, Eddie, no I won't,' I said quietly.

'You bloody will or you'll be in jail before morning!' he snapped.

The stench of him was overwhelming, and the thought of putting *that* in my mouth made me feel sick. He was a vicious man though, and he grabbed hold of my hair, wrapping it around his fingers to keep my head in place. He started to push himself towards me, as I tried to move my mouth away from the thing he was forcing on me.

'Suck it,' he kept saying, 'suck it!'

I was shaking my head and telling him 'No, no!' but he kept trying.

'Suck it! Suck it like a bairn's bottle,' he hissed at me.

I just couldn't do it. Holding my hair and head, he kept trying to force me to take him in my mouth. He was getting more and more excited, but he couldn't hold on to me, hold on to himself and force my mouth open. Instead he started rubbing himself on one side of my neck, then the other. After a while, as I sobbed, he let go of my hair and grabbed both of my wrists in one of his hands.

'Hold that,' he commanded, shoving his penis at me again.

I was so scared that he would do something to hurt me, but I was also completely repulsed by him. I was still in agony, my stomach cramping constantly, and I prayed that someone would come to the bathroom door and notice it was locked.

Eventually, someone did rattle the handle. Eddie was still rubbing himself all over my hands; I didn't know what he was leading up to but he stopped to listen when he heard the noise at the door.

'Someone in there?' came a man's voice I didn't recognise.

'Shut up!' whispered Eddie to me. 'Aye!' he shouted in the direction of the door. 'I'll be done in a minute.'

'Hurry up, man, some of us are desperate out here!' came the reply.

I heard footsteps walk away as Eddie told me to get up, get myself sorted and stop 'greeting'. The tears did stop, because I saw that there was a chance for me to leave the bathroom without anything else being done to me.

Eddie opened the door, cautiously, and walked out, holding me in place behind him. No one was there. No one saw us leave.

The party was still in full swing, and Eddie went back to the living room, leaving me, dazed and alone, in the hallway. A few minutes later, Gerry appeared.

'All right, wee Sheena?' he asked, as always.

What could I say? What could I ever say?

'Aye, Gerry,' I whispered. 'I'm fine.'

Chapter 7

Memories

All of this happened before I was five years of age. My memories aren't complete, because I was so young, so sometimes I have no idea of what happened in between the visits to Auntie Betty and the encounters with Eddie. Life must have just gone on as before. I'd be back with Granny Morag, and desperately wishing for my mummy to come for me.

It is the weekends I remember. Perhaps I don't have them all in order, but I do recall what happened depending on what else was going on at that time. So, I know whether I was at school or not, whether it was near to my birthday or Christmas, whether Mummy had sent me new clothes or whether I was still in rags which my granny would dress me in.

So much had happened to me even before I turned five but, one day, I decided I had to tell someone properly. Unfortunately the person I chose to tell was Betty again, Eddie's sister-in-law and the woman who had brought him into my life as well as keeping him there. I had told her before, on the night that I couldn't sleep with the pain in my wee bum, the night after he had tried to rape me and I was still bleeding hours later. She had dismissed me then, told me to be quiet and never say a word against him, but things were getting worse. On top of that, I blamed myself – perhaps I hadn't told her properly last time?

I remember that I just blurted it out one day. I was so young that I didn't have a plan; I just couldn't keep the pain and the hurt inside me any more so, on a weekend when I was at Auntie Betty's, it all came pouring out. I hadn't seen Eddie yet on that visit but, as always, my stomach was churning at the thought of what might happen. I never knew when I would see him, sometimes he would come to Betty's, sometimes he would be at the bus stop when I got off but, always, always, he would be there on every visit I made.

I was standing in Betty's hall, taking my coat off, when I spoke up immediately.

'Auntie Betty,' I said.

'What?' she snapped.

'I don't want to see Eddie this time,' I went on.

'What are you talking about?' she asked sharply.

'I don't want to see him. He's not nice,' I revealed.

'Rubbish. You'll see whoever I say you'll see. Nothing wrong with Eddie,' she concluded unconvincingly as she started to walk back to the kitchen.

'Auntie Betty!' I called out.

She sighed and turned round.

'What?'

'Eddie's *not* nice, he's not.' I paused. 'He hurts me. That's not nice.'

'What do you mean, he hurts you?' she asked, coming no closer to me. 'You're a bad wee lassie – if he skelps you when you're naughty, that's your fault, so you needn't think you can tell tales on him.'

'No ...' I replied falteringly. 'He hurts me ... different.' I didn't really have the words to tell her. 'He hurts me ... here.' I pointed to the front of my dress, beneath my tummy, the place I had no real name for but where Eddie was always fumbling and touching and making sore. 'My wee bum. He hurts my wee bum.'

Betty narrowed her eyes at me. There was no sympathy there but I so wanted her to believe me, to cuddle me, and to say that I wouldn't have to see Eddie again.

'He does, Auntie Betty, he does,' I whispered. 'It's really sore and I don't want him to do it.'

She stared at me.

'Liar,' she hissed. 'Liar. You're a nasty little liar and I'll be telling your granny that you're a nasty little liar. Never say things like that about Eddie. Never.'

With that, she walked away from me, and I was left to wonder what to do next.

Betty kept her word. When I was taken back to Granny Morag at the end of that visit we'd barely got in the door when Betty called out to her mother (who was never one to rush and welcome me home), 'Mum! You're not to believe a word Sheena says. She's been telling all sorts of tales about Eddie, absolute rubbish. She's a liar, Mum, a liar.'

'Is that right?' asked Granny, finally coming through and looking my way, burning her eyes into me.

'Aye,' Betty continued. 'Right wee liar. Says Eddie's been touching her and hurting her. It's all lies, Mum, she's a liar.'

'Aye, she is that,' said Granny Morag.

They both left me there and went to put the kettle on for a cup of tea. When Betty left, a while later, she repeated the lines she had been so keen to say as soon as we arrived.

'Remember, Mum – she's lying about Eddie.'

'I'll remember,' replied Granny. 'You leave her to me.'

I didn't know what to make of this – I had been telling the truth, I had, so why was Betty calling me a liar and why was she telling Granny not to believe me? There was so little I understood about my life, so little I actually knew about what was really going on with Eddie, that I was always confused about what the grown-ups were doing. However, the things which I knew for sure about my life I held dear to me. I knew that my mum had gone to America to work. I knew that she had been back, but that she had gone away again – without me. I knew that I loved her and I knew that I would never stop hoping she would come for me.

The social work department made their regular visits. Every time they came a great show was put on. Granny would say how hard she worked, how she was having to do more than she should at her age, but also what a martyr she was in that she would never leave me to fend for myself, despite my own mother doing exactly that in her version of the story. 'That poor child,' she'd say every single visit, 'dumped on me by her own mother. But never you mind,' she'd say more to the visitors than to me, 'I'll be here for her; I won't leave her on the streets.'

As an adult, I know that my mum wasn't even in the equation. She had been airbrushed out of her own daughter's life, and Granny was now my mother in the eyes of the law. As I've said before, she was paid for this and, to be honest, I think that was why she did it in the first place. Money was always important to her, for its own sake; she didn't spend much of it on me, as Mum always sent me parcels of beautiful clothes and toys, but the steady trickle of money from fostering me would have been important to Granny.

I don't think we were actually poor as such. We certainly weren't rich, but there was a culture of penny-pinching and generally being very 'tight', which made everything feel more poverty-stricken than it was. Granny reused everything, she never threw anything away, she never really had nice things around the house, and she was always warning us all about ending up in the poorhouse. I think a lot of working-class people back then had a fear of absolute poverty and worried that if they allowed themselves to splash out on what they saw as luxuries (even though they weren't really that) they would be on a slippery slope to rack and ruin.

I wouldn't have had many toys or any nice clothes if it hadn't been for Mum sending them from America. Granny Morag always had money squirrelled away, but it wasn't for me, not even the amount she got for being my foster mother. I remember my fifth birthday happening sometime after I told Betty about Eddie hurting me. I don't know how much time had passed, probably a couple of months.

'You can have a party,' said Granny Morag.

I was so excited! Turning five was a big thing; it seemed very grown up to me, but having a party all to myself was even bigger. Everyone around us, all of the other farmers and farm workers and their families, came to the party, and they all gave generous gifts, as did my favourite uncles and aunties. They all brought food too, no doubt because they realised that they'd get nothing much at our house. I was given so many presents by them all and was deliriously happy. None of them came from Granny Morag though and some of them don't really make any sense thinking back – for example, I clearly remember a Huckleberry Hound toy dog which was filled with dolly mixtures, but I can't for the life of me now work out where the sweets were kept, as the dog seemed like a solid toy.

One of the things I loved in our house was the old wind-up gramophone we had and, for my birthday, I was given some new records. My favourites were always Danny Kaye and Bing Crosby and Doris Day, because, to me, they represented my dream world, the world of Mummy: America. What I really wanted though, was her – and that was exactly what was missing. I was still terrified that if I didn't 'fix' things for Eddie I would be jailed, as would all of my family, but I was starting to think more of escape. If Mum came back I wouldn't have to worry about jail or ever 'fixing' Eddie again, because she would rescue me, she would take me back to America where everything would be safe and we'd be together for ever. It was the dream that kept me going for many years, but there was something else going on in my life which brought a huge change. I was going to go to school soon. I think that the time of before-starting-school and after-starting-school is a big change for any child, and it certainly focuses memories for me. Just before I began school something happened to me which is confusing to this day.

When I say 'something happened', I'm not trying to be deliberately evasive; I genuinely don't have all the details. I just know that after 'something happened' I ended up in hospital. I do know that there was a party, as there often was, at the Johnstones, and I was planning to stay over, along with Betty, Charlie and Tracy. The night was progressing as it normally did – there was a lot of drinking and a bit of arguing but then, all of a sudden, all hell broke loose.

I could hear it all from the bedroom where I had been sent to sleep, and Betty had come through with Tracy not long after – I think she had sensed something was about to kick off because she told me to just stay quiet for a while. It was impossible to sleep properly, given the noise, so I was lying there, a bit dozy, listening to the adults getting louder and louder. Betty was in bed, Tracy was in a bassinet, and I was in a sort of cot bed near to the window.

That weekend, one of Charlie's other brothers, Malcolm, had made an appearance. Malcolm had split up with his wife and turned up just as the party started. He had expected to stay over, but Gladys told him that Charlie and his family, including me, were in the room he expected to use. That was the room they had stayed in while they lived there, and they still had quite a lot of stuff in it. Malcolm seemed put out by this immediately and the drink had obviously made him more vocal.

I could hear lots of shouted insults from him, aimed at his

brother and mother, and by the sounds of things it was getting violent. I could hear them in the hall outside the bedroom, then they all came piling into the room, with Charlie and Malcolm punching each other. I stood up in my cot bed to see what was going on and the next thing I knew I was flying across the room.

That's actually how it felt to me. I thought I was flying. Of course, what had happened was that I had been picked up and thrown – by Malcolm – but I had no direct memory of that at the time. I know that he was telling me to shut up and that Betty was crying, telling him to stop, begging Charlie to do something, but it was all hazy. I was in pain and people were screaming. I had landed at the bottom of the wall on the opposite side of the room and there was a shooting pain going through my arm.

After that I remember waking up in a hospital bed. I was in the children's hospital – or the 'Sick Kids' as we called it – and my shoulder was in a harness. I had been through surgery without realising it, and the whole family had been waiting for me to wake up. Malcolm had been thrown out, and was actually sent to Carstairs some years later (the very place which Eddie threatened me with) for another violent attack.

My head wouldn't stay up straight – when I tried it fell forwards or sideways or backwards, something was wrong and I didn't know what. Had Malcolm lifted me by the head and wrenched the muscles? Whatever it was, I had been traumatised. I've tried to get my medical records, but have been told that they – like my social work files – have mysteriously disappeared. I do remember the harness very clearly. It had a leather head-piece with chains attached to either side. It went over my chest and shoulders and had to be put on by someone else. Everyone was very concerned. While I was in hospital they all came to see me and I loved the attention as well as the presents. I was visited by the whole Johnstone clan. Auntie Betty came in with her kids, with old Gladys, with kind-hearted Gerry – and with Eddie. I was in shock really. I didn't know what was going on as the doctors hadn't said much to me (it just wasn't the 'done thing' to tell children what was going on in those days). I was in the hospital bed one day, in my nightie, as the whole Johnstone side of the family traipsed in. There was a lot of fussing with everyone saying 'poor Sheena' and giving me sweets and suchlike, but Eddie just hung back behind everyone, saying nothing and watching me.

After a while Betty's kids started playing up. She dragged them out of the ward and called for Gerry to come with her.

'I'll take them outside for a bit of fresh air,' she said. 'Settle the wee buggers.'

'I'll come as well,' added old Gladys. 'I could do with getting out too – I hate hospitals. They give me the heebie-jeebies.'

'I'll stay,' said Eddie. 'I'll make sure she's all right.'

'I'll stay too,' said Gerry quickly, glancing from me to his brother.

'No, you go,' hissed Eddie. 'Help Betty with the weans. Go.' He stared at his younger brother, and I knew that Gerry wouldn't have the strength to stand up to him. I was shaken out of my stupor by the thought of being left alone with Eddie but at least knew that he wouldn't try anything on in the middle of a hospital ward.

As soon as they had all left, he moved closer to me, sitting down on the hard plastic chair at the side of my bed.

'You feeling fine, Sheena?' he asked.

I nodded.

'I think I'll try and sleep now, Eddie,' I whispered, childishly hoping that would be all it would take for him to leave me alone if indeed he did have any plans. I looked around the ward to try and assure myself that there were others there, that I wasn't alone. About half of the beds were occupied, and there were people sitting beside most of the patients.

'You do that,' he replied. 'You do that.'

I wriggled under the thin sheets and closed my eyes. I heard him drag the chair a little closer.

'It's very busy in here, Eddie, isn't it?' I said, my eyes popping open. 'There are lots of people, aren't there?'

He stared at me then a slow smile crept across his lips.

'Aye, wee Sheena, you're right there – are you finding it hard to sleep?'

Before I could answer, he stood up and pulled the curtains half closed on each side around my bed. He didn't shut them entirely – I suppose that might have drawn attention – but just enough so that the top half of the bed, where he sat and I lay, was obscured.

'There – that's better. Much more ... private,' he smiled. 'Now, you just close your eyes.'

I did as I was told, praying that, if I could convince him I was asleep, he'd leave me alone. Around me, the conversations continued, the sounds of children talking to and laughing with their families went on – I hoped against hope that Betty would be back soon, but I suspected she was taking her time, having a cup of tea, smoking, leaving Gladys and Gerry to look after the kids.

I felt his hands creeping under the covers, searching out my body until he found what he was looking for. I kept my eyes screwed tightly shut the whole time and didn't make a sound. Why? I don't know. No one had ever believed me in the past and I can only think that, even there, even in hospital, I assumed that I would be called a liar had I brought Eddie's actions to the attention of the nurses.

No one noticed a thing as he kept poking and prodding me with his fingers underneath my nightdress. I concentrated on the sensation of the dressings I had on – there was one in particular which was pulling at my skin and I tried to make my mind think only of the feel of the tape around the edges which was catching on me and giving me a slight irritation. If I only thought of that I could get through this just as I had so many times in the past.

Suddenly he stopped touching me and I heard him speak.

'Is that better, Sheena?' he was saying, too loudly. 'Are you comfortable now?' He was plumping up my pillows and re-arranging the sheet.

'Has she got you running round ragged?' Betty said, as they all congregated around my bed again. 'Proper little madam, isn't she? Never happier than when she has everyone at her beck and call.'

Eddie laughed quietly. 'It's no bother, Betty,' he said, 'no bother at all.'

'You're a good man, Eddie,' she replied as my stomach

lurched. 'Thank Eddie then,' she said to me. 'Thank him for being so nice to you.'

He leered at me, raising his eyebrows and winking, out of sight of the others as he continued to fuss around me.

'Say "thank you, Eddie" if you know what's good for you,' commanded Betty.

'Thank you, Eddie,' I parroted weakly.

Betty sighed. 'Say "thank you, Eddie, for being so nice to me" – Christ, do I have to tell you everything?'

'Thank you, Eddie, for being so nice to me,' I repeated.

'It's like getting blood out of a stone,' she complained. 'Right, everyone – let's get going.'

With that, she gathered up their things and ushered her children out of the ward without another word to me. Eddie was last to go.

'You're very welcome,' he said to me as he left.

I closed my eyes and turned away from the door as they all disappeared. A few seconds later, Gerry was at the side of the bed.

'Take care, Sheena,' he said, planting a shy kiss on my forehead. 'Take care, wee one.'

I could feel the tears form in my eyes as I heard Eddie shout 'Gerry!' from the corridor. Gerry left and I was alone with my thoughts.

I didn't often get visitors as everyone in my family was working or had other things to do, and the novelty of me being in hospital soon wore off. Over the next few days I kept a close eye on the other children in the ward, particularly a little girl in the next bed. Every time she had visitors, I would look over, often through half-closed eyelids as I pretended to sleep. I was trying to find out if she had an 'Eddie'. I never saw anyone doing anything to her. She would get sweets and be brought gifts. She was always happy, and it never went mysteriously quiet, her curtains were never drawn, she was never left alone with a man.

I was on the lookout for *it*, to see who else *it* was happening to. I was always so sore from what Eddie did to me, and it was that which made me think it was wrong. I didn't think he should be hurting people. I didn't know it was sex, I didn't know what sex was, and I had certainly never heard the word 'abuse' – I didn't think Eddie's attacks on me were wrong because of any of that. I thought it was all wrong because it was so painful.

While I was in hospital I was never checked 'down there', they just focused on my neck. I suppose they had no indicators that I was being abused and people were less aware of the whole topic back then. On top of that my granny and everyone else took every opportunity to remind all and sundry – doctors included – that I was a 'fantasist'.

I heard them say it to lots of people and had even heard the usual words being trotted out one day to a consultant who came to chat with me when Granny Morag was there.

'You know, she comes out with some stories, this one,' Granny insisted on telling him. 'She says terrible, unbelievable things about folk – don't you believe a word if she starts.'

Looking back, it was obvious that she was getting her point of view in first, just as Betty did, so that, if I ever did tell, she would have already put the thought in their heads that I was a liar.

When I went home I was still in a harness. There were no more operations after that but there were a lot of exercises, what would be called physiotherapy now, I guess. I had to keep turning my neck, putting it on my shoulder, slowly bringing it back again, and strengthening it. There was no investigation into why it happened, Granny and Betty never had to tell me to shut my mouth as I didn't really remember anything. I think I must have been knocked out and my main recollection was that I was flying. Literally flying. I went across the room, I know that. I used to say to people 'I can fly, I can fly you know!' and I used to believe it myself. I also thought that, now that I had managed it once, I could do it again. If I could truly fly, I could fly to my mummy. I tried. I tried so hard. I would sit on my bed with my eyes closed concentrating. I was cross at myself for not being able to do it because I was still so desperate for her, and now I thought it was only my own lack of talent in the flying department stopping me from going to America and being with her.

I was still waiting for her.

I've always waited for her.

There was something inside that made me want to be with her, no matter what I was told. Granny said she didn't want me. She said that, if Kathleen wanted me, she would have come and got me. I was told that Mum had made a new life and just left. I was told that she had married an American man, Bob, and was probably going to have new babies. They would be her real family.

I was just something she had left behind.

One day I looked out from the kitchen window and saw

Granny hanging the washing out. We had a washhouse in those days. You lit the fire under the water to get started, and my usual job was to put everything through the wringer including the big sheets. Granny had put them in the big wooden tub, washed them, then put them through the wringer herself as I was still in a harness, then she hung them out. She'd gone through most of the process and was now trying to catch the thin sunlight to dry them. Something in me must have thought this was a good opportunity to talk, so I went outside.

'Granny,' I began. 'When I was in hospital, something happened.'

She said nothing, so I went on.

'When you all went out one day, Eddie was there with me alone.'

There was still no reaction.

'He touched me in bad places, Granny. He touched my wee bum.'

Quick as a flash, and without warning, she turned round and slapped me.

'I wondered when this would start!' she shouted. 'Shut your mouth! You hear me? Shut your mouth.'

I started to cry.

'Crying because I've called you out on your lies? Well, keep on the way you're going and you'll be crying a damn sight more. Betty warned me, she warned me long ago about you and I know what you're up to. You're trying to cause rows between Betty and Charlie, aren't you? You don't like the fact that they're together, do you? You want Betty for yourself, you want her as your own mother after yours abandoned you, don't you?'

It wasn't true. I didn't want that at all. No one could replace my own mummy; I just wanted someone to believe me about Eddie, but it was clear that Morag and Betty had decided that this was the line they would take, irrespective of what I said.

I had no one to rely on. No one to turn to for protection. No one who would believe me.

However, I did have something to look forward to – I was a big girl not long after the accident and I was starting school.

When I went there for my first day, I was still in the neck harness. Before I started school I didn't really have friends because there weren't many people where I lived. There were sons and daughters of the farmers but they weren't meant to fraternise with the labourers; we were much lower down the social scale and things like that mattered back then. To be honest, I didn't really want to see other children; they scared me because I didn't know how to behave around them. I was never sure whether making friends with anyone while I was at Betty's might mean they would come to Eddie's house for me and he would end up hurting them. I couldn't protect everyone, so it was easier not to have friends.

Granny was becoming more and more horrible about Mum. She seemed to take a lot of pleasure in telling me that things were different now – I was fostered by her, Mum had met a new man and then, one day, that Mum was having another baby. A new one, one she would keep. That hurt a lot, but I tried to concentrate on the good parts – soon, I would have a baby brother or sister!

'Don't be stupid,' Granny said, when I mentioned this. 'You're just the wee bastard she dumped. This is what your life is now. She'll keep this one, you mark my words – and you? You'll just be a bad memory.'

Chapter 8

This is what your life is

But Mum didn't forget me. She continued to send beautiful things. That was what I held on to when Granny Morag was telling me that Mummy didn't love me. If she didn't love me, why did she always remember me and send gorgeous gifts?

Sometimes I would get toys, sometimes I would get little things such as ribbons to put in my hair, but what I usually got was clothes. Fresh, fancy clothes which were different to anything the other girls wore. My outfits from America made me so proud. I used to daydream about how they had been chosen with love and care. I thought of Mum thinking of me – and the bond which connected us every time she bought me a new dress and posted it to Scotland. When I opened the packages I believed I could smell her. I would hold the clothes to my face and think of her. It was magical.

Granny Morag couldn't complain because my mum's gifts meant that she never had to spend money on clothes for me. That woman took tightness to a new level and she would do anything to save a penny. The outfits were clearly expensive, so she was doubly happy – she saved money and I was also well turned out. I may have been filthy, I may have been smelly, but I had beautiful clothes.

One weekend, when I was sent to Auntie Betty's, I was wearing my newest gift from Mum. It was a skirt of red, white and blue stripes with little flowers on top of the striped cotton. The white T-shirt had matching flowers and there was a matching bolero jacket. I had white plastic jelly sandals, and white socks with flowers on them and a scalloped edge. She had even remembered to send matching knickers – again, white with little blue flowers. I was beside myself with happiness. I thought I was the bee's knees and all of it had come from my lovely mummy.

Granny Morag put me on the bus to Betty's and I sat there like a little princess. I didn't think there was a better dressed wee lassie in all of Scotland.

'Look at you all fancied up!' said Betty with a rare smile when she saw me (it was also rare that she was the one to meet me). 'Very nice!'

I was so happy that day. The clothes were beautiful, but, more importantly, they reminded me of Mum and that was what mattered most. How could I believe she had stopped loving me when she sent such thoughtful gifts?

It wasn't long before Auntie Betty found something for me to do; you were rarely idle in our family. Betty used to get what we called 'tick' off a shop a few streets from where she lived. She would get the goods she wanted and the shopkeeper would keep a running tally of how much she owed him, which would get paid at the end of the week when the wages came in. People were paid cash in those days, certainly for manual labour, and there were no credit cards. This was just the way it worked. If you ran out of money, you got food on tick and you made sure you paid it on time or you'd never get credit again.

It was just a fact of life. There was no embarrassment or shame to it as lots of people were on the breadline and shops needed to be a bit flexible to survive when times were hard. Back then, in the late '50s and early '60s, children were also given a lot more responsibility and, even at a young age, would be sent to shops for the 'messages'. If they could carry them, they could be sent for them – that seemed to be the rule! It wasn't unusual to see wee tiny things struggling up the road with bags of shopping (and usually their mum's fags in their pockets too).

That day, Betty shouted to me as I played in the hall of her house.

'Sheena! Go down to Patten's for me and get a few things!'

She would have paid off her tick book the day before when the money came in, and now she was right back on the same cycle of debt, getting prepared for the next week. I ran through to her to find out what she needed. I liked to keep busy when I was there to keep away from Eddie if at all possible and, on this occasion, it was summer so I was there for even longer. Sometimes, I'd be there for weeks on end. It didn't matter how long I was staying – ever since Eddie had started abusing me, a day or a few weeks were all the same to me in terms of the effect it had on my nerves and stomach. When it was time to go, I felt as if I was walking to my doom. I got sick, had diarrhoea, and was generally so ill at the thought of being at his mercy that I would shake. It got me away from Granny Morag's violence, but it just took me to another place of danger. There were good parts to staying with Betty; I loved her mother-in-law and the great spreads of food she laid out, I loved Gerry and his gentle ways, but I hated the bad things.

Betty handed me some message bags and a notepad – on the pad was a list of what she needed and a note to say that she wanted it all on credit. I trotted off to Patten's the grocer, and got everything on the list. It was standard stuff – eggs, bread, milk – and I began the walk home with the two shopping bags laden with food, trying to be careful and not mess up my new clothes.

I hadn't walked very far when Eddie appeared. I hadn't seen him coming as I was concentrating so hard on carrying the messages.

He said nothing to me.

He just appeared there, in the street, and stood in front of me, forcing me to stop.

As I looked up at him, I could see he was agitated. He was always like that before he abused me. He seemed to get himself worked up. It was as if his thoughts were taking him to a place where he had to go forward with what he was thinking. I don't know how much control he had. At first, I thought that he might be going to help me with the shopping. I was really worried about whether I could get the eggs in particular back to Betty without breaking them. But my hope soon faded.

He just kept staring at me.

I tried to walk a few steps, but he continued to block my way.

He looked around – there was no one else paying attention; the few people on the street were going about their own business.

'Come here,' Eddie said, grabbing me by the wrist and taking one bag off me.

I whimpered at the pain he caused me, and held on to the other bag with all my might. I assumed that he was going to drag me back to Auntie Betty's or his mother's house. I also assumed that he was going to abuse me once we were there. Even if Betty was still at home, he would take me into the bathroom and I knew better than to make any noise.

He had a different plan that day.

A new approach.

And one which was worse than anything he had done before.

Just off the street we were on was a smaller side street where, a few hundred yards down, was the public convenience where he had started abusing me when I was only four. We had been back there many times and I hated the place with a vengeance but today, as he pulled me in, he was even more worked up.

'Eddie!' I cried. 'Betty will be looking for me! She'll wonder where I am – she'll want her shopping!'

He looked at me with cold, hard eyes.

'Betty sent me for you,' he snorted. 'She won't be looking – she knows you're with me. Now, shut the fuck up.'

He was panting and getting more and more excited.

If he was going to do anything – which I knew he would – I expected him to take me into one of the two cubicles and lock the door. But he didn't. Right there in the middle of the men's toilets, he started touching me. He seemed so angry and I wondered what I had done wrong.

'What is it, Eddie?' I asked. 'What have I done?'

'Shut it! Shut it!' he shouted, seemingly oblivious to the fact that anyone could walk in at any moment. There was such venom in his voice that I felt he really hated me.

'Get down,' he snarled.

Where? Where was I to get down? What did he mean?

I must have looked confused, because he got even angrier, then pushed me onto the floor. He was threatening and vicious and nasty. He pushed me onto the floor then pulled my pants down. It was a cold floor made of cement. There were bits in the wall for men to urinate in – one on one wall, two on another – and two lockable cubicles. I could see it all and I prayed for someone else to come in, but they didn't. It was just us.

Eddie sodomised me that day.

I couldn't scream because he held his hand on my mouth and I was choking. He had his hand over my mouth and my nose and I couldn't breathe properly.

The pain was horrendous. He ripped me in two and I thought I was going to die. I didn't see how I could stand the level of pain he was putting my tiny body through.

On top of everything all I could think was:

I need to get this shopping back to Betty . . . I need to get this shopping back to Betty.

I was concentrating on his fingers on the hand I could see. Eddie was a pipe smoker and he made his own roll-ups too. His fingers were stained from the nicotine; the smell and taste of him was disgusting.

He had one hand holding me down, one hand on my face. When he pushed himself into me, he pulled his hand around. His fingers were trying to get inside of me as he was having trouble doing what he wanted. I had landed on the shopping and I had heard the eggs smash under me.

'Shut your fucking mouth,' he kept saying, but I couldn't scream anyway.

He was squeezing me tighter and tighter, squeezing my nose, squeezing my throat. The next thing I knew, there was the big grunt and the noises he always made – like a pig. That's how I used to cope with it sometimes. I used to imagine he was an animal, but I couldn't distract myself that day.

Finally, he let me stand and pulled my pants up. They were ruined. All of my beautiful clothes were ruined. He didn't even try and clean me up. I remember the terrible pain when I started to walk up the road to my auntie's house. I was crying and the eggs were broken and leaked into the bag.

I had wet and soiled myself with fear.

I will never ever forget walking 'home' with the blood and mess in my clothes and the smell of him on me.

All I could do was wail quietly as I walked. I could see people walking past but no one did anything. I was making a noise like a banshee, but no one cared.

I knew 'it' had gone into a different place this time but, as always, I had no words for it, no conception of the fact that he had just anally raped me. Although he had poked around at my bottom before, he had never attempted to put his penis into me there – this was a new horror.

'Where the hell have you been?' shouted Betty when I finally walked into her house.

I couldn't even think of how to tell her what had gone on. I could barely even stand. I was in agony. Shocked. Shaking. Unable to really process what had happened. I didn't have the words or the maturity to know what had gone on. The only thing I knew was that it was the worst thing that had happened to me yet, and that was saying something.

'Look at the state of you!' she shrieked when she saw me. 'What the hell have you been doing? Jesus! Look at the eggs – have you smashed every bloody one of them?' she screeched. 'You've broken all of my eggs! What are you standing there for? Tell me what you've done? Why did you do that? Why did you break my eggs?'

'I can't . . . I don't . . .' I stammered.

'Speak up, you bloody dimwit,' she said. 'Spit it out. Explain yourself!'

'It wasn't me . . . I didn't do anything . . .' I started to explain.

'Of course it was you, you wee liar!' she retorted. 'You've smashed the whole bloody lot of eggs! What were you doing? Playing? Skipping down the street?' She peered at me. 'Christ, look at the state of you!'

I was filthy. My clothes were ripped and torn. My face was dirty and streaked with tears.

'Auntie Betty,' I began. 'A bad thing's happened . . . I've messed myself, I've dirtied myself,' I whispered.

'I'm not blind, I'm not stupid and I can smell you!' she shouted. 'I suppose you just expect me to clean you up, do you? Wash your fancy bloody American clothes that your fancy bloody American mother sent for you?' Betty always said this about my mum when she was angry at me – it was as if she didn't even acknowledge that she was talking about her own sister.

'Well, you've got another think coming. You can stay in your own filth all bloody weekend for all I care . . . actually,' she went on, 'you can sort yourself, you dirty, smelly wee bastard. Get up those fucking stairs and get washed.'

'Auntie Betty, it wasn't my fault . . . it was Eddie . . .' I whispered.

'You fucking liar!' she screamed, slapping me across the face with the back of her hand. 'Why are you always telling lies? Why do you have it in for Eddie? I'm sick of your stories, sick of you making things up. I take you here out of the goodness of my heart to give Mum a break from you, and you pay me back like this?'

'No, I'm telling the truth, Auntie Betty, I really am. I didn't break the eggs, it was Eddie when he grabbed me. He hurt me really bad this time, he truly did,' I told her.

'Liar! Liar! Liar!' she said, slapping my cheek each time she said the word.

I tried to tell her, I honestly did, but she wouldn't listen. It was as if she just didn't want to hear what I was saying.

There was no question as to why a child that age would have been in such a state. It was all my fault and I was a dirty wee bitch, according to Betty.

When it was time for me to go home that weekend, Betty took me and, just as she had on the previous occasion when I had told her about Eddie, she informed Granny that I was a liar as soon as we stepped in the door. She had barely spoken to me all weekend, apart from hissing 'Liar!' at me every time she passed me, and I had spent the few days in agony as my little body started to ache even more from the horror Eddie had inflicted on me.

Betty also started to tell anyone who would listen that I was a liar, that I made up stories, that I lived in a fantasy world. I'm sure that this was to cover herself. All my life she said I was someone who lied.

After that first day, over time, Eddie raped me anally about a dozen times. And the pain was awful and something that I never got used to and I screamed as loudly as I could. He would order me not to but it was agonising. Eventually, I would just let him do it while the tears ran down my face, but I always screamed when he started as I felt that my body was going to rip in two. I never got used to that. I soon learned that no one would come and I just needed to get through it – the faster he got on with it the sooner it would be over. That was the most I could hope for.

Chapter 9

That little girl

Eddie continued to abuse me, but it was always pretty much the same. The weekly sessions were times when he would either penetrate me or force me to relieve him with my hand. I suppose I was becoming better trained. I didn't bleed so much, although it still hurt, and I knew that the threat of jail was there constantly, even if he sometimes used it as a threat without much enthusiasm. We both knew each other well by that stage. I knew that he was an evil bastard and he knew that I would never be believed if I told anyone what he was doing.

There were some times when I did refuse, but they were few and far between. Eddie had pushed me into a cupboard underneath the kitchen sink once, and that had worked – I had been terrified and compliant then and, given that I was still so little, the tactic worked every other time he tried it too.

At one point, some work was being done in the bathroom in their house. The bath was an old-fashioned one with claw feet and there was a wooden panel being placed along the front to try to make it more modern (this sort of thing was done a lot –

lovely, original features were ripped out of houses as a matter of course and replaced by ugly-looking things which everyone thought were the height of fashion). The panel was loose and things were being stored behind it. To begin with, there were tools and suchlike, but as the job went on and showed no signs of finishing, all sorts of junk was put behind there. The panel itself could slide along and this must have given Eddie an idea.

We were in the house alone and he wanted me to 'fix' things by taking him in my mouth. As I've said, this was the act I most hated. It wasn't just the smell of Eddie which disgusted me, it was the fact that he seemed closer than ever. On top of that, I was beginning to think that the white blood wasn't blood after all and that it didn't really hurt him when it came out. Although he made lots of noises when I was 'fixing' him he always seemed to recover very quickly. I wondered whether he was really ill, whether he was really in pain, at all? I knew that when bad things happened to me, it took ages before I felt better, but Eddie's recovery was instant, as soon as the white blood came out. Whatever it was, it smelled just as bad as the rest of him. I carried it around with me and I often thought that everyone else would be able to smell it too.

So when Eddie attempted to get me to do that horrible thing that morning, I had shouted 'No!' and run from the living room. This was unusual for me. I rarely defied him, never mind shouting and running away.

He chased me down the hallway. 'I'll fucking nail you in there if you don't fix things!' he shouted.

I was terrified – there were spiders, which I was petrified of, and I really thought that if he put me in such a place I might never come out. When he caught me and dragged me back to the bathroom, I was barely on my knees at the bath panel before I gave in. He always won.

I have very few photographs of myself as a child, but there is one which breaks my heart. I must be about seven years old and it has been taken by a professional photographer. This was simply the way back then. There were no digital cameras or supermarket printing in those days. On special occasions people would go to a studio and sit for a posed picture. I remember that I was taken to a shop in Edinburgh's Leith Walk for this snap. In it I am sitting on a white basket chair with a patterned cushion behind me and a fake backdrop of clouds on the wall. I'm wearing one of the outfits which Mummy had sent me from America – a pleated skirt and sleeveless blouse with a sprig motif, white ankle socks and sensible shoes. My hair is quite short, my legs crossed at the feet and my hands clasped together.

There is nothing remarkable about the black-and-white photograph apart from what I know was happening to the child with the shy smile who looks back at me. The abuse from Eddie Johnstone was so severe that the innocence of the picture hurts me to this day. I just want to reach into it and save that little girl. I wish I could grab her and run a million miles away from the man who had robbed her of her childhood. It's too late for her, the past can never be changed, but I see so many missed opportunities in the image, so many people who could have helped and who chose not to, or who put themselves first.

Whenever I got home after a weekend with Betty and the rest

of her in-laws, I would count down the days until I had to go back. If it was term-time I knew that I would have until the next weekend, but if it was during the holidays I had no idea when Granny Morag would just suddenly announce that she'd 'had enough' of me.

Even when I did get home on a Sunday night the thought of school the next day was no comfort. I had no friends there and I was being bullied. Actually, I'm not surprised. The biggest problem was that I smelled. I smelled really badly. It wasn't just that I wasn't washed very often. It was worse than that. I smelled of *him*. He was at me so much and he was a filthy pig of a man. He never washed and he smelled like old cheese, like Stilton. I've never eaten cheese since the time came when I could make my own choices about food. It reminds me of him too much. I tell everyone that I'm allergic to it, but it isn't true. It's a trigger for me, a way of allowing the bad memories to flood back in that I have to avoid to keep myself together.

I knew that the smell was like Stilton, because that was a treat my Granddad enjoyed and even when it was him eating his favourite snack I had to leave the room because it was too reminiscent of Eddie's horrible stench. His smell was all over me and the other children knew it. They may not have recognised what it was but they understood that I was rank.

We didn't have a bathroom in the cottage and all washing had to be done in a tin bath. In theory, bath time was meant to be once a week, but it all depended on Granny's mood and whether she could be bothered to wash her charge. Having to bathe in the tin bath in the kitchen meant no privacy, but we didn't really have any of that anyway. The kitchen was basic with a Belfast sink and a worktop with curtains on wire underneath to act as makeshift cupboards. In the corner was a flushing toilet but the door never closed as there was a cooker wedged in beside the wall and the gas cylinder sat inside the toilet. There was no privacy even when going to the loo, and when any of the men went it stank the house out.

I could only have a bath if Granny was having one. She went first so I knew that I would be next and that the water would be cold. Afterwards, the laddies would carry it outside to empty. I was never really clean. I may have had lovely clothes from Mum but, underneath, I was filthy.

The other kids would say I was 'humming', and they'd go about sniffing the air dramatically, asking what the stench was whenever I passed by. I'm paranoid now. I shower at least twice a day and I'm always checking to see if I have any body odour at all. Some things never leave you.

The bullying was sometimes physical. There were occasions when half-a-dozen boys and girls would get around me and shove a lot; they'd push me to each other. I hated the physical contact but I bore it, always wondering why they didn't like me. It was my fault, I smelled, I knew that – but couldn't they see that I was a nice person?

No one seemed to be able to see anything good about me. I believed that everything was my fault – with Eddie, with school, it was all down to me. I was a bad lassie. Everything was wrong because of my badness but there were happy moments in my life too. It's impossible to have an existence which is completely unrelenting and there were funny times too. I remember one night when Granddad came back from being out drinking with his friends. He came rolling in, singing and shouting for his 'wee darling'.

'Shut up!' came Granny Morag's voice from her room. 'You shut up, you old drunkard! Get to your bed and leave the rest of us in peace!'

But he had other ideas. I heard him continue with his love songs as he made his way to the forbidden territory – Granny Morag's own, solitary bedroom which he never slept in. I heard smooching noises as he kissed the air and told her what a wonderful woman she was. Then I heard something I couldn't quite understand but which made my aunties in the room with me split their sides with laughter.

'What about my needs?' he was saying. 'A man's got feelings, Morag – a man has . . . he has . . . well, he has *conjugal* rights, you know!'

'I'll give you fucking conjugal rights!' she screeched.

It made me laugh so much!

I could hear the pair of them – him in her room, trying to get all romantic, and her shoving him away, shouting, 'Get off me, you dirty bastard!' I tell you, he must have been a brave man, my Granddad, to even try and get soppy with that woman!

We all got up and waited in the living room. Granny came through to where we were all holding our sides, trying not to laugh out loud at the pair of them. Granddad was still hanging on to her, making smooching noises, and telling her she was a gorgeous woman. As they both appeared, she fell over a big iron weight we kept the door open with. She went all her length onto the floor and he landed on top of her.

'See?' he shouted. 'See, Morag? The gods are with me! I'll show you a good time now, lass!'

She was squealing like a stuck pig.

'Will one of you lot get a stick and hit the dirty bastard over the head?' she shouted.

'Aw, Morag – don't be like that,' he said, still trying to get a kiss. 'It's high time we enjoyed ourselves; we've done nothing in that department for years! I'm a man, I've got needs! You're my wee darling, so you are, come on now, let's show the young ones we've still got a bit of life in us.'

'Life? I'll give you bloody life! I'll brain you when I get my hands on you!' she retorted.

I was helpless with laughter. It was one of the funniest moments I could remember. When things were like that, it was lovely, but those times were few and far between. That night, seeing that he would soon be on the receiving end of something other than my Granny's romantic side, two of the boys put Granddad to bed. In his own room. He had a big metal bed. I loved it there, I'd jump about and have a lovely time. He was a good man and I loved him dearly. I remember once getting in and cuddling in to him. I knew he was completely safe but it still took a lot for me to do it, because I'd been so damaged by Eddie by that time.

He smelled nice too. He smelled of soap and cream shaving soap.

But Eddie? He smelled awful, there was always a stench

coming from him. It never changed, and neither did his need to abuse me. He never seemed to lose his appetite for what he did. He must have done those things on hundreds, absolutely hundreds, of occasions. I was at Betty's every week while I was very little. The only other place I ever got sent to was a sister of Granny's and the worst thing that ever happened there was that I was forced to eat tomatoes! However, Betty's house was the stop-gap. That was my second home really.

Sometimes he would even abuse me more than once a day. I couldn't believe the first time that happened. Generally he would start on me as soon as he could encourage Gerry to leave. Each time Gerry would try and find an excuse to stay but he was no match for his brother, and Eddie always won. Once he had abused me, once he had ejaculated, everything would be normal. Or it would look normal. Of course, behind that facade of 'normality' was a totally dysfunctional family, but things calmed down at least after Eddie had done what he wanted to do. He would sit down afterwards as if nothing had happened and read the racing pages.

I'd be left alone, physically aching, often crying, and certainly confused from what had been done to me, and Eddie would chat as if it had never happened.

'What do you think then?' he'd say. 'Do you think that horsey will win for me today?' He'd say the name of whatever racehorse he was looking at. 'That's a nice name for a horsey, isn't it?'

I'd look at him blankly while he waited for a 'normal' response.

'You'd like a horsey like that, wouldn't you?'

Again, he'd wait for me to act as if everything was fine.

'Aye, Eddie, aye, I would,' I'd say.

'Well, I'll maybe get you a horsey one day. Aye, maybe I will,' he'd reply, nodding, content with his empty promises to a broken little girl.

I have to admit, it shut me up too. He would promise me a horse when I was bigger, or he would promise me days out to the seaside, and it would make me think of the good things rather than the trauma he was actually putting me through.

I know now that many abusers are very good at that – even when they are doing the most awful things imaginable to a child, they are also reeling them in, making promises and offering some light in their lives. The irony is that when Eddie did talk about getting me a horse, I thought he was wonderful. I was in the most awful pain – emotionally and physically – but when he stopped and acted 'normally', I would wonder what was going on and just focus on the dream of a horse or the story about a day out. It was as if the way he acted afterwards was sending me a message about how I should be too. This method of carrying on with normal routine after touching, raping or getting me to do things to him was necessary in terms of him hiding it of course – he couldn't risk drawing attention to what was going on – but it also made me think *Maybe that's just how life is. Maybe these things happen to all wee girls.* Certainly, given the behaviour of many other children around me, that wasn't such a deluded view of the world as you might think.

The pain – the physical pain – was getting more bearable, simply because my little body was becoming used to the ravages inflicted on it. You get used to anything eventually.

Eddie was often alone in his mother's house and he would always, always, take advantage of that, but he would also abuse me when other people were there. There were often parties and at those parties people were always drunk. They simply wouldn't notice the disappearance of both of us. The bathroom was where he preferred to do the bad things. When you walked along the hallway (the lobby, as we called it), you turned a corner and the bathroom was immediately ahead. If I was sleeping over at that house, the bedroom I used was directly opposite it. This meant that even if I went to 'my' room for something he would follow me, drag me into the bathroom and do whatever he wanted. On other occasions, when I went to my bed, he would also announce that he was having an early night. He'd follow me and, yet again, get me on my own.

There were signs if anyone looked for them, but they didn't. By the time I was about seven I had developed a habit of compulsive hand-washing. I was forever doing it – skirtling in the sink was how it was described – always trying to get clean. I suppose I knew that I could never get a feeling of cleanliness, but I could keep trying, trying, trying with my hands. I could focus on them, try to take control of that one part of my body.

My time there was falling into a pattern. I'd get there at half past eleven and he would send Gerry away. I'd be abused and then he would make some food for us both. The truth is, I liked it when he was in charge of meals. He would go straight to his mother's biscuit box and pile a plate high with chocolate treats, which were usually only for the adults. In those days if you were poor it was unheard of for kids to have free rein over any food, and certainly not over chocolate biscuits. So, on days when I was suffering the most unholy things I was also rewarded with biscuits and sweets, and that is what I learned to concentrate on. I hated the Eddie who hurt me but the Eddie who gave me treats was wonderful.

And there were always treats to be had. Even though we had very little money – certainly, in comparison to now, we would have been seen as living in poverty – we had more than many and there did always seem to be cash (or tick) for things like those chocolate biscuits, bottled beer for the men and Sweetheart stout for the women. Granny Morag always had a quarter gill of whisky on the go and she liked a dram in her tea. It was about the only thing that made her happy – that and her Consulate fags! That woman smoked like a chimney and she was famous for it. I still have an image in my mind of her standing at the sink, peeling the tatties, a fag hanging out of her mouth (she always had one in there – I used to think she had a dent in her bottom lip to rest it!) and a big dottle of ash hanging off the end. Those lengths of ash could get to some size in those days as the cigarettes were of different quality, and we would all take bets on when it would fall off! If it fell in the tatties that was just tough luck – 'added flavour' she'd say!

The house was always full. People always came to Granny, she was there for them all. If they got chucked out of their house for not paying rent, they came to her. If their man was hitting them, they came to her. It's hard to imagine because she had such different sides to her. She could be wonderful and warm and helpful, but she could be evil. If she liked you, she liked you, and she'd bend over backwards, but if she didn't your card was marked and you could never get her to change her mind. I think my card had been marked since the moment my mother left. She was taking it out on me, I'm sure of that, but the irony is, there was no need. By this time Mum had two more children in America and seemed to have forgotten all about me. There were still parcels and there were still memories but I was starting to believe Granny Morag – I was just the little girl who had been left behind.

Chapter 10

Family

By the time I was seven Betty and her husband had three children of her own, all born in quick succession. Tracy was three, Arthur was two and William was a baby. I felt very grown up when I was with them – they seemed like little babies to me, whereas I was a big girl. They kept Betty busy. If she had ever been the slightest bit aware of what was going on with Eddie, she hadn't shown it; and now that she had three children of her own I was all but invisible to her.

I can't understand why Eddie did the things he did and I also can't understand how people allowed it to go on. I had often told Betty that he was hurting me but she was more concerned with telling people that I was a liar than getting to the root of the problem. However, she and lots of other people nearby left their children with him. Perhaps it was because of Gerry, I don't know. He was such a gentle man, so good with wee ones, and children were drawn to him. Eddie exploited that and he made his own brother's life a misery too. Yet, as a mother and grandmother now myself, I cannot for the life of me work out why on God's Earth Betty risked leaving her babies with that man.

One day Eddie and Gerry were looking after all four of us at Betty's house. I had just arrived as I'd been at school that week and when Betty announced that she was going out she left her own children too.

'Be good!' she shouted breezily as she headed out the door. I have no idea where she was going. She spent a lot of time with friends, she went to bingo, she socialised. I don't know what was so important that she felt she had to leave her own flesh and blood with that monster, but she did. I could understand her leaving me to some extent – after all, she'd never shown me any warmth – but her babies? Nothing will ever make me understand that.

Eddie was very keen to get rid of Gerry that day.

'Take the weans to the park,' he snarled.

'Aye, Eddie – all of them?' asked Gerry.

'No – leave Sheena and wee Arthur,' he replied.

Gerry hesitated before saying, 'It's a bit cold out there, Eddie. I think I'll just stay here – with them all.'

'No – you won't. You'll take them to the park just like I told you to,' came the reply.

Gerry wasn't smart enough to come up with excuses and he was frightened of his brother, so off he went with Tracy and the baby, William.

I sat on the floor, playing with two-year-old Arthur. I was aware of Eddie watching us but I tried not to look at him or talk to him. I foolishly thought that I could make myself invisible and he would leave me alone.

Arthur got a bit grizzly after a while, and I was worried that it might bother Eddie, who was still silently watching us, so I tried to pick him up. It's tricky for a seven-year-old to manoeuvre a two-year-old who is wriggling and cranky and Eddie offered no help.

'He needs his nappy changed,' he told me.

It might seem odd to readers now but I had changed Arthur's nappy in the past. Betty had shown me how to do it since, as I mentioned, she was always looking for ways to get out of doing things herself. I wasn't terribly good at it, and it was a cloth one (there were no disposables back then), but I could try. I'd rather do that quietly than be there with Eddie getting cross.

'Come on then, wee Arthur,' I cooed to the boy. 'Let's get you sorted.'

I started back towards the rug in front of the fire where we had been playing, with Arthur still struggling.

'No,' commanded Eddie. 'Not there. Take him to the bathroom.'

My blood ran cold. The bathroom in Betty's house was where he often took me when the abuse happened. He would lock the door and no one was any the wiser. I hated that room and didn't want to go in there when he was around.

'It's fine, Eddie,' I said. 'I can do it here. Betty's shown me how to do it, I can manage.'

'I don't care what you can and can't do,' he snapped. 'I told you to take the bairn to the bathroom, and that's what you'll do.'

I got to my feet, knowing better than to argue with him any more, and gathered Arthur in my arms.

He followed us.

'I can do it, Eddie,' I said again.

'Aye, so you keep saying. Well, you won't mind if I check now, will you?'

I did mind. I minded a lot, but I couldn't do anything about it.

He pulled the door closed behind us and locked it. I lay Arthur on the floor and sat down beside him. In Betty's house the bathroom was downstairs. You weren't in direct line of it from anywhere else in the place, so it was where he often took me if anyone else was around as there was very little chance of being spotted.

'Take his nappy off,' he stated. 'Take it off.'

'I know, I know,' I muttered.

'Take it off,' he said again, getting more agitated.

Then a thought hit me.

Why was he getting so worked up about this?

I may have only been seven, but I wasn't stupid.

'Take it off,' he kept repeating. 'Take it off, take it off.'

I did what I had never done before. I screamed holy murder. There was no way I could hurt a baby and no way that I could be party to whatever perverted notions Eddie had with regard to Arthur. I knew that he wasn't wanting me to change the nappy any more. He had something else in mind. I was just a little kid myself – but a two-year-old?

'Take it off,' he said again.

'No, Eddie, that's bad, it's bad.' We both knew what I meant. We both knew I was referring to what he wanted to do to little Arthur.

'Do it,' he said.

'No,' I whimpered.

'Do it. He's dirty. Do it.'

'No! No! He's not dirty, Eddie, he's not. I don't need to change him now – I've remembered. His mum changed him just before she left. Honest, she did, Eddie. I'm telling the truth.'

'Shut up and do it . . .' he said.

Just then, I heard the front door slam.

Gerry.

'Gerry!' I shouted. 'We're in the bathroom! I'm changing Arthur's nappy – Gerry!'

I heard him run along the hall towards us. Gerry knew more than anyone gave him credit for, and I'm sure he knew just what Eddie would be planning given that he had us both in there.

Eddie threw the door open just as his brother got there and I pushed past him, Arthur in my arms, tears running down my face.

Eddie looked at his brother and neither of them said a word. Gerry and I both knew what Eddie was but we were bound in silence by some strange family loyalty. Tracy and Arthur don't even talk to me these days. Like their mother before them they won't admit to the horrible things that went on at the heart of our family. I know, and they know, what Eddie did – and they no doubt know what else was going on. He wasn't just abusing family members, he was inflicting his perverted behaviour on other children too. I often walked in on him when there were others there and I often saw him pulling his trousers up or felt my heart sink as he shouted out that I wasn't to come in yet.

What I can't understand is *why* there were always children there. Why did parents allow it? I know that there will be excuses – some will say that times were hard and mothers needed a rest, that they didn't have anyone to help them and were grateful for some time off. There will be those who will claim that a woman's work was never done, that they spent all of their time washing (without machines), cleaning (without machines), and cooking (from scratch). That may very well be the case but it is no excuse, in my mind, for allowing their children to be abused.

Eddie was not a nice man. That may seem obvious, but what I mean is that he didn't even have a veneer of charm. Many paedophiles cultivate a persona for other people if they are abusing children outside of their immediate family. They may appear to be generous or kind, they may be charming and friendly. Eddie was none of those things. He was smelly and uncouth. He was unpleasant and vile. He wasn't attractive in any shape or form. Even if he *hadn't* been an abuser, I can't see why any parent in their right mind would have entrusted their child to him.

The village in which I lived and the one in which Betty and all of her in-laws lived was neither sophisticated nor educated. People did work hard, and they had little to show for it. There was nothing outside of their small lives really and I wonder whether there was just an acceptance, a tolerance of things, which other communities would have found abhorrent? Looking back, there were so many children who displayed overtly sexualised behaviour and that is something which I found odd even then, even before I had the words to describe what was going on.

There was a family who lived next to Granny Gladys called

the Millers. The children were very provocative, very sexually aware. The little girls – of all ages, younger and older than me – would stand up at the window ledge inside their house, take their pants off and hold their vests up. They would rub their bottoms at the folk walking by. Had Eddie abused them? What made them act that way and why did their parents not stop it?

The children from another family – the Finlaysons – were just the same. I can remember when one of their boys knocked me down on the grass and said he was going to 'shag' me. I was seven and he was about ten. I know that lots of children use words that they've heard without necessarily understanding the meaning of them but, as Ricky Finlayson said that to me, he held me down on the ground and tried to push his hands inside my knickers. He was thrusting himself on me in a parody of adult behaviour and saying over and over again what he was going to do.

One of his sisters came over and dragged him off me. She started hitting him and crying, saying, 'You will not, you will not!' It was very odd and, in retrospect, I feel there was a whole community of abused children in that place. Perhaps there was a paedophile ring, which would make some sort of sense as it would explain why people weren't bothered by Eddie and why they continued to leave their children with him, despite him being such a horrible and dangerous man.

The behaviour of so many children was just wrong. Children were left with him all the time and he touched a lot of them; where did it all end? Who was involved? As a child I thought that those other kids were just doing what I called 'bad play' but as an adult I wonder about it. I think there were more adults than Eddie involved – if those girls were standing with their pants down and vests up in front of the window, their parents must have been in the living room behind them, not bothering. Why was that the case? Where had Ricky learned to behave like that and why was his sister so upset by what he was saying and doing to me?

The kids next door to Granny Morag had older girls but some of the younger ones were peculiar. They all seemed to be into sexual talk, talking about which child was 'shagging' which other child. It was far too advanced for kids. There was no sense of them joking about it or using words they didn't understand. It was as if they were having an actual conversation about things that were going on.

At that time, when I was still about seven, new houses were being built near to where I lived and this group of children all talked about the girls 'shagging' the workers, and that if we (the younger ones) went up there we'd see it all happening. It was beyond normal childish talk and I wanted no part of it. The things being done to me by Eddie were enough horror – I had no inclination to witness what someone else may be going through.

I suppose, in many ways, I'm putting this all together now as I write about it. The parents must have known there were more kids than just me being abused. Those children were all too sexualised and all too easy for him to access. I keep going back to the same question – why did people continue to trust Eddie, leaving children with him? One of the answers could be that he wasn't the only one; maybe they were sharing children. I wasn't there all the time.

The abuse was intensifying but, looking back, the most

appalling thing about it all was that I was expecting it to happen. Even though I was only seven I knew that every time I was sent to Betty for the weekend, or for holidays, he would be there and IT would happen.

I didn't know it was sex, I didn't know it was related to sex, because I was too young to have that awareness. When you're brought up on a farm, you see sex all the time, but that doesn't mean you necessarily relate it to what humans do, or what grown-ups get up to. The animals in the fields and the pens and the barns did what they did, and there were piglets and calves and lambs as a result. Children would see what happened as the seasons passed, but it was all natural, it was just part of the circle of life. It never struck me that the things Eddie did were related in any way. He never said it was sex – and of course, as an adult, I know that it was so very different from any normal, healthy sex which normal, healthy people engaged in – and I didn't link it that way either.

What I did know was that I hated it and that it always happened. There had never been a time since it started that I had gone to Betty's and he hadn't abused me. It was as if that first time had broken the barrier and now it was just what Eddie did to me, and what I accepted.

From the day he had tried to make me take him in my mouth, I had dreaded that so much. As I mentioned, he always looked filthy and I was never aware of this changing. If he washed, if he tried to keep clean, it was never when I was there. Baths tended to be something that only happened once a week when I was a child, but I doubt whether Eddie was even as regular as that in his washing habits. Every part of him smelled and when he had been at me I stank of him. The fact that he ejaculated on me so often and seemed to take pleasure in doing so meant that I was always aware of the stench of him. When he had forced himself into my mouth I had gagged and been unable to do what he wanted, but that hadn't stopped him trying time and time again. I'd never managed it. The smell of him was so overpowering that I would dry heave as soon as he put his penis close to my mouth. I knew it made him angry but I couldn't help myself.

One Saturday afternoon, as I was playing with my cousins, Betty shouted through from the kitchen, a place she seemed to spend most of her time.

'Sheena! I'm needing milk!'

My stomach churned. I knew what this meant. Betty always seemed to need something from the shop, and because she had her little ones to look after and was pregnant again her default option was to send me to Eddie's house. As always, I would be given money and a list and told to get Gerry to take me for whatever Betty needed. I wasn't trusted to be sent to the grocer on my own since the time I broke the eggs. They must have thought more about the welfare of their groceries than of me, as I was regularly trusted into the home of a paedophile.

I've often wondered just how much Betty knew. She was certainly keen to promote the lines my Granny Morag spun to everyone, and they would both denounce me as a liar and a fantasist at every opportunity, but did she actually know how bad it was? I have no idea, and I'll never get the answers to so many of my questions. But I do know that every time she called on me from the kitchen my heart seemed to stop beating.

'Get your arse down there,' she said. 'There's the money and there's the line.' She threw some coins and a bit of paper at me.

'I can go myself, Auntie Betty,' I said. 'I'll be good, I won't lose the money.'

'No!' she snapped back. 'Get Gerry to take you. I need more than milk; he can carry it. Now, piss off.' She pulled me up, roughly, and shoved me out of the front door. I stood there on the step and wondered if I could risk it – could I go to the shop on my own? Could I hand the money over, get the things Betty wanted and dawdle about for a while so that she thought I had been to Eddie's? Then, when I came back, surely if she had what she wanted, it wouldn't matter that I'd gone by myself?

The door opened behind me.

'What are you standing there for? Get your gormless arse off there – and don't hurry back.'

I shuffled down the street, knowing what I was walking to, knowing what would happen. Or, at least, thinking that I knew these things. Eddie had already abused me that weekend. He had met me from the bus as usual and kept to his tried and tested pattern, but I suspected that wouldn't be enough. If I turned up, like a lamb to the slaughter, he wouldn't turn down the chance.

When I got there, Gerry opened the door to me.

'Hello, wee Sheena!' he said. He always looked so pleased to see me but he was such an innocent man that he could hide nothing. I had started to notice that after his initial pleasure when I turned up his face always clouded over and looked sad. In retrospect I know that Gerry was aware of so much of what was going on, but he did what he could, and he was never bad to me, or to anyone else.

I heard Eddie's voice from inside. 'Is that Sheena? Bring her into the kitchen, Gerry, hurry up!' he called.

Gerry took my hand and closed the door behind us. The house was quiet and I couldn't hear anyone else.

'Have you to go for messages, Sheena?' asked Gerry. 'Does Betty need something?' I nodded. 'Come on then,' he said, squeezing my hand even more tightly, 'let's go down the shop.'

'Not so fast,' snapped Eddie. 'Leave her here; she's no good to you anyway. Slip of a thing like her – what's she going to carry? She can wait with me, Gerry; you go get what Betty wants.'

'No, no, Eddie,' he said, gently but firmly. 'I'll take the wee lass with me. It'll be fine. It'll be fine.'

'I've told you once and I won't tell you again. Leave her here. Now – go.' He pointed towards the door and Gerry kept his eyes down.

'I'll just take her with me, Eddie, I'll take the wee lass with me,' he insisted in his quiet way. I didn't hold out much hope – Eddie always got what he wanted. I knew that better than anyone. 'I'll take wee Sheena, I'll take her.'

Eddie didn't even bother to reply. He simply pushed his brother towards the door and shoved him out into the street. He turned back to look at me. 'There,' he said, with a horrible finality in his voice. 'Just you and me.' He started to walk down the hall to the kitchen as I stood, stock still, hoping he wouldn't ask me to follow. Still with his back to me, he stopped. 'Silly me,' he said. 'We're not on our own. I forgot. Callum's here – come and meet him.'

I didn't know who he meant. Who was Callum? Even at such a young age I knew that Eddie was playing me. He hadn't forgotten that this Callum was there; he never did anything by accident – everything was planned. Was there a man here that I didn't know? Would he help me or hurt me? I had no way of telling, no way of predicting anything.

'Come and meet him,' Eddie went on as all of these thoughts flew through my head. 'Come and meet Callum.' It was an order, not an invitation.

I walked obediently behind Eddie as he went into the living room, only to see, not a man, but a little boy of about three or four years of age. I didn't recognise him, but there were always so many children in all the houses nearby that I may very well have seen him before.

'Come here,' Eddie snapped, and I began to walk over to where he stood at the fireplace. 'Not you,' he said, 'him.' He pointed at the little boy. 'Come here, Callum.'

Callum jumped off the settee and went over to Eddie. The boy didn't seem scared – in fact, he seemed perfectly at home, as if he had been there before, and as if he knew Eddie well. I had no idea who he belonged to but he was a skinny wee thing, with mismatched clothes and a dirty, unkempt look about him. 'Do you like him?' asked Eddie, looking at me while holding on to the boy at his side.

'What do you mean?' I replied.

He sighed as if I was a real bother to him. 'Do you like Callum?' he repeated.

'I don't know him.'

'But do you like him?'

'He's too wee to play with,' I said with the pride of a seven-year-old who didn't want to have to play baby games.

'I don't want you to play with him,' said Eddie. 'I want you to touch him.'

I didn't really know what he was saying, and I didn't have time to process it, but I just knew this was bad and I wanted no part of it. 'No!' I shouted immediately, much louder than I had done in a long time. 'No, I won't!'

'What do you mean you won't?' he scoffed. 'Who put you in charge? You'll do whatever I fucking tell you to do. Touch him. Touch Callum.'

'I'm not doing it,' I said, quietly this time. I tried to back away, towards the door, praying that Gerry had forgotten something and he would be back soon. He knew I was there and I suspected he knew what Eddie did to me, and he must have known Callum was there. Perhaps he would make an excuse to come back and that would stop the unnamed horror I felt was facing me. Throughout this exchange Callum said nothing. He'd picked up a crust of bread from a plate lying at Eddie's side and started to gnaw on it with the intensity of a small child.

'Will I get you started?' Eddie asked. To my disgust he knelt beside the boy and pulled down his tatty shorts. This perverted, filthy beast grinned at me all the time.

'Come on, Sheena,' he said. 'Touch him. Touch him like you touch me.'

I know to this day what was going through my mind. When

Eddie touched me it hurt. If I touched this little boy I would hurt him. I didn't want to touch him. I didn't want to hurt him. It was wrong to hurt children; I knew that even if it didn't seem to apply to me. I wouldn't do it, I *couldn't* do it. He was so little, so pathetic and obviously uncared for, and there was no way I could add more misery to his life. The boy just stood there as Eddie went on to pull his pants down.

'There,' he said. 'Suck that. Get it in your mouth – even you should be able to manage that.'

I remember two things – the first was that there continued to be absolutely no reaction from Callum, and the second was that he was so young there was hardly anything to see. Eddie was holding the little boy's private parts in his hand and I thought that there was a world of difference between the horrible thing he forced on me, and that of this little boy.

I wasn't going to change my mind. *Nothing* could make me hurt that child. I didn't care what Eddie did to me or what punishments he would think up, all I wanted was for him to leave us alone. 'No, no, no! I'm not doing it! I'm not doing it!' I screamed.

He rushed towards me and, for the first time, hit me. The force of his hand across my cheek made me stagger backwards but, as I did, I could see Callum pull up his pants and trousers and toddle back to the settee, still munching on leftovers he'd found lying around. Eddie kept saying that I needed to do as I was told and I kept refusing. The pain in my face and my ear where he was continuing to wallop me was excruciating but I would have taken it a hundred times over to stop him touching Callum or forcing me to touch him either. Somehow, I managed to get out of the living room. As I headed for the front door I shouted, 'I'm running away, Eddie! I'm going to get Gerry!'

I flew out into the street and ran for only a few hundred yards before I saw him, the brother who was safe, the brother who was a good man. I threw myself into his arms and he set the shopping bags down on the pavement to hold me to his chest. I was sobbing my heart out and Gerry just said over and over again, 'It's fine, wee Sheena, it's fine. Gerry's here. Gerry's here.' He didn't ask what had happened and I didn't say. Even then, I knew that this gentle giant didn't have the capacity to understand much but he did seem to know that I needed him to just hold me.

After what seemed like a lifetime, we went back to the house. It was as if nothing had happened.

'Did you get Betty's things?' Eddie asked when we entered the living room. Callum was sitting on a chair, drinking a cup of milk and eating a biscuit. He wasn't crying. He wasn't upset. In fact, he looked perfectly content. I wondered how many times he had been there before, and what hideous things this awful man had inflicted on his tiny body. 'Callum's mother will be here soon to pick him up.' He looked straight at me as he said the next words. 'He's been as good as gold – he can come again. Maybe it'll be easier if it's just me and him, what do you think, Sheena? Peace and quiet – that's always best.'

That day was the first and last time Eddie hit me. He had found my limit. I wouldn't do this, I wouldn't hurt another child, I just couldn't. But it wouldn't stop him trying again.

Chapter 11

Loss

I always felt protective towards Betty's children but I never knew what happened to them when I wasn't there. Ever since that day when Eddie had tried to get me to take Arthur's nappy off so that he could abuse him, I had a new worry. I didn't just have myself to protect – not that I was very good at that, there was very little I could do – but there were these three innocent souls in his line of fire too.

Despite that I wouldn't say I was close to Tracy, Arthur and William. When you are abused, self-preservation is all. Even when there are others to look out for, it's dangerous to make links or show weakness through being open about how much you care, because that can be another way for the abuser to exert control. I never discussed any of this with Betty's kids, they were too little anyway, but I also suspected that, even if they had been able to talk about it, like me, they wouldn't have wanted to. Sometimes keeping the horror to yourself is all you can do to get through.

But sometimes the horror becomes even worse than your worst nightmares.

About a year after the 'incident' in the bathroom I was at the house of Granny Gladys (I had to call Betty's mother-in-law and Eddie's mum 'Granny' as well, just as most kids in those days had to call adults 'auntie' or 'uncle' or any other family title when there was actually no blood link). As usual the women were out – probably at bingo – and Gerry had been sent to the park with Tracy and William. I have no idea whether Eddie had been abusing Arthur or the others by then but as soon as it was only the three of us in the room he put his hand down the little boy's trousers.

It was deliberate.

He was showing me that he could do whatever he wanted. Arthur didn't even seem that surprised, and he wasn't upset or crying, so I can only think he was used to it by then.

'Don't do that, Eddie,' I said. 'It's not nice. Leave the wee boy alone.'

He smiled and removed his hand.

'Fine,' he said.

I breathed a sigh of relief – then watched in horror as he took Arthur's trousers off and put his hand down the boy's pants instead.

He started moving his hand about in there, and I felt sick. I needed to stop it. I needed to save Arthur.

There was one thing I could never willingly do, despite Eddie trying to make me do it so many times. I could never, ever let him put his penis in my mouth and not feel sick. He was a filthy, smelly bastard and any time he tried I gagged.

Something inside me changed that day. Maybe something

died. I realised that I would do anything I could to survive and, at that moment, to save that little boy.

'Come on, Eddie,' I said, 'come with me. Come through to the bathroom and I'll sort you. I'll make it better. I'll fix the bad thing.'

I led him by the hand to the bathroom and gave him oral sex for the first time on my own initiative.

I was barely eight years old.

It was the first time I had managed to do it, but I needed to save Arthur.

And did it work? It worked that day, but I wasn't there all the time. Arthur died when he was ten. The doctors said it was peritonitis. His bowel ruptured and his insides were poisoned. Was that because of the abuse? I think so. In my heart I know it was, but that man was never brought to justice and an innocent child died.

I was losing so much. I didn't really have a childhood. For someone to deliberately take your innocence is an appalling thing. You don't even have a life when you grow up because you're so used to *that* happening that you'll sleep with anyone because that's what you've been taught. You have no self-respect, no love for yourself, you don't know how to fall in love as half of that is desire and that is the part which has been twisted. Everything is filtered through the abuse and conditioning you've had, and becomes all about giving a man gratification. As a child you're just relieving men, love has been taken out of the equation, it's all messed up and that stays for ever. You don't know what normal sexual desire is so it's never real, and the pattern for that, for me, was set in those early days.

I knew in a way that it was a wrong thing as he said not to tell anyone, and I knew how I felt when I thought he was going to do it to someone else but by that time I had been told so often that I was nothing but 'a fucking liar', 'a wee bastard', 'an evil wee cunt', who deserved to get her 'fucking arse broken' that I really believed I was worthless.

I think that the Johnstone family was completely dysfunctional and a lot of it was because of inbreeding. Someone later told me that Gladys had married her own cousin and that they rarely went outside of their own blood for husbands and wives. It certainly seemed to run deep, because one night Charlie Johnstone – Betty's husband – climbed into bed beside me too. She was at bingo and he was watching the bairns. I was in a single bed nearest the wall and Tracy was in one under the window, asleep. Charlie climbed in behind me – he must have thought I was dead to the world – and tried to put his penis between my legs. I threw my arm back and dug it into him.

'Uncle Charlie, get out of here,' I said dozily, pretending I was more asleep than I was and giving him a get-out option, hoping with every shred of me that he would take it.

'Oh, oh, I thought I was in my own bed,' he said, flying out of the room as quick as his legs would carry him

It ran wild through that family. I don't think Charlie hurt his own, I think it was as if I was fair game because I didn't have a mummy. I had no one looking out for me.

I had given up listening for aeroplanes by this point. I knew that Mummy had some new babies and I felt that the best I could hope for was that she would keep sending me nice toys. I wasn't sure that I wanted the pretty clothes because they seemed to just draw Eddie's attention to me even more than anything else, but I loved the games and books and comics – especially the comics. I had the first editions of everything and wish I had kept them all, because they did give me pleasure and kept me going through some very hard times.

One day, when I hadn't even heard an aeroplane, she arrived. I still thought that when she came I would hear the roar of the engine and then she would be there moments later but that didn't happen at all – instead it was a taxi not a plane. There was an old man on the farm who ran a taxi and I heard it that day. I was never told in advance that Mum would be coming for a visit. By that stage things were awful with Eddie. He was abusing me so much that it was something I just expected. There was never a visit to Betty's where he didn't get me. I was always sore, always aching, either internally from what he was doing to me, or physically from the pain of him holding me down to do whatever he wanted. On top of that I was hit regularly by Granny, and there were very few people showing me any genuine affection on a regular basis, apart from Gerry. My youngest auntie, Rose, was lovely but Granny Morag hated her, so she stayed out of the house as much as possible to avoid the wrath of her own mother. Two of my uncles who still stayed at home – Freddie and Robbie – were nice too, but they worked all the hours of the day and they weren't Morag's favourites either. Her eldest daughter by Big Kenny – Nellie – and her youngest child by him – Jed – were the ones she loved. She was very open about caring for them most, but it did mean that the children who were kinder and nicer to me stayed out of their own mother's way as much as possible as she had little time for them. Nellie and Jed may have been her favourites, but they didn't have that status with anyone else. They were completely indulged by their mother and it had turned them both nasty. They could get away with anything they liked and never face the consequences. Granny Morag didn't seem to see what she was doing – she didn't ever have to face the consequences either from what I could tell.

So, on the day that Mum appeared, I was losing hope.

'Old Taffy's taxi's there!' I shouted to whoever was in the house. 'Someone must be coming – I'm going to see!' I didn't think it would necessarily be someone for us, but any visitor to any of the farm cottages was a welcome distraction.

I couldn't believe the vision that got out of the car. She was like a film star. She was beautiful, just beautiful. Her hair was such a light brown that it was nearly blonde; it was perfectly styled and she had on a matching dress and coat jacket. She looked like Katharine Hepburn. She was like no one else's mother I had ever seen.

I was crying with joy from the start.

I was saying 'Mummy, Mummy' over and over again.

Granny came outside immediately with a face like thunder.

'Get inside,' I was told, but I ignored her. Mummy smiled at me and then looked at her own mother, her face darkening. I skipped round to all the other cottages to tell them the wonderful news. She was here! She was here!

By the time I got back – everyone seemed delighted for me – the atmosphere was even more strained. I didn't care. I had everything I wanted. Mum hugged me briefly, once, but there was not the amount of kisses and cuddles that I had dreamed of. Maybe she had been gone for too long, maybe there were too many other people there, maybe the proximity of Granny Morag was too overwhelming – I don't know, but I do know that it wasn't what I had been dreaming of. It was wonderful that she was there – but I was never left alone with her, not for a second. When I asked her later that day why she hadn't come before, I caught a look between her and Granny. The old woman had a defiant set to her face and nothing was said.

She was withdrawn and subdued on that visit. I wanted to sleep with her, but Granny said she had to share her bed. I didn't mind too much. Why would I? I thought I would be going back to America with her soon.

She was there for two weeks, two whole weeks. Every time I was in the room Granny would make some comment.

'Missing your kids, Kathleen?' she would ask. Then, just as quickly, she'd answer herself, 'No, I don't suppose you are – you find it easy enough to dump them, don't you?'

Mum never rose to it when I was there, but I have no idea what went on when I was at school. I couldn't wish the hours away quickly enough so that I could get back home and just breathe her in. She lost some of her shine while she was staying with us – I bet she noticed that too; I bet she saw what she would become very quickly if she stayed around.

Then, one day, when I came home, she was gone.

Gone.

Without any warning.

'She's good at that,' cackled my granny as I sobbed my heart out. Then she melted a little, no doubt seeing that she could work this to her advantage. 'You poor wee soul,' she cooed, giving me a rare cuddle, which I accepted gratefully. 'Dumped again. Heartless, that's what she is, heartless.'

I hated her then. I hated my own mother. She'd barely hugged me; she'd never even tried to be alone with me from what I could tell. Morag was right; I felt abandoned all over again.

There were cracks appearing everywhere. I wasn't the only one doubting someone I loved. Auntie Betty had been absolutely devoted to her husband and his family (at my expense) but now something was going wrong there too. I do believe she had been genuinely in love with Charlie and this is why she kept their secrets, but flaws had been appearing in their marriage ever since they moved to their own house. With three very young children and a man who liked the drink more than family life, her patience was running thin. Not only was she seeing a manipulative side to him, he was battering hell out of her too. Back then, if a man was a good provider and handsome he was a catch. Charlie was both of those things. He looked like Rhett Butler and he worked at two jobs, but then he started to knock her halfway into next week on a regular basis. They were starting to argue a lot in front of other people, and Betty was also staying over at the farm cottage a great deal with the kids.

Perhaps because I was getting older I was just noticing things. Eddie was still at me constantly when I was there, but I was also beginning to pick up on other things. I once walked into the kitchen behind Eddie when his sister Celia was peeling potatoes (there was always someone peeling potatoes in every house). Instantly, she swung round at him, oblivious to the fact that I was there, with the knife in her hand.

'Don't come near me!' she screamed.

'I wouldn't touch you with a fucking bargepole,' he snarled, turning round and pushing past me to leave.

Lots of little things were falling into place but not really making sense yet – I still couldn't see the full picture; I still didn't know that this wasn't normal, that not all families worked this way. All I knew was us and the Johnstones. The only other person who was really in my life on a regular basis was the social worker.

Every time he came Granny would start her usual litany against me. 'What am I supposed to do with her?' she'd ask. 'She comes out with some awful things, you know, terrible lies.' She always got in there first – just in case. The social worker was usually a man and he'd lap it all up.

'I'm having a terrible time with her, we'll have to do something,' she'd go on. 'You've never heard the likes of what she'll say about people.'

I remember him saying in reply, as clear as if it were yesterday, 'It's just her age, Morag, they go through this, especially abandoned kids. The ones who have been thrown away by their mothers are the worst. Terrible liars, every one of them; I see it day in and day out.'

He didn't care that I was sitting there. There was no consideration for my feelings at all.

'You'll find, Morag,' he'd go on, 'the ones who get dumped

have this fantasy life, and it can sound very realistic to those who aren't in the know.'

He was setting himself up as an expert, but I'm sure he thought I was spinning tales about having a princess for a mum and a rich family with yachts, not a paedophile in the family. Whatever the reason, he like everyone else seemed blind to what was going on in my life and what was being done to me. What I had lost and what continued to be taken from me was something I could not express and no one else seemed to have any interest in saving me from the horror that was continuing every time I went to visit Betty.

Chapter 12

Light at the end of the tunnel

As time went on I started to make excuses. I hadn't been listened to when I was very young and said that I didn't want to go to Betty's. From the time I was about eight I got a little respite. I was getting bigger, so perhaps other people were more willing to look after me now and again. I would tell Granny that I fancied staying with Teresa for the weekend – her sister who always made me eat tomatoes, always forgetting that they made me ill. It was a price worth paying. Maybe Teresa hadn't wanted me in the past, but by the time I was eight or thereabouts I was a good wee worker and I could help anybody out around the house. They farmed cattle so they appreciated the help. She was very house proud, so was even quite happy if I just spent the weekend polishing her huge kitchen table until it gleamed, as that was one less job for her to do.

Sometimes, as time passed, I could get away with only going to Betty's once every three weeks, then once a month. It was never longer than that, but there was relief in those days away from the threat of Eddie.

My abuse by Eddie stopped when I was nine years old and Betty moved house. I simply had no reason to be in his world any more. I don't think he cared who he abused and he always seemed to have access to many children, so there was no need for him to follow me to Betty's new address and try to get to me there. I doubt whether he gave me a single thought in the years that followed. I was just one of many and there seemed to be a steady procession of victims for this horrible man.

I remember when it dawned on me that the horror might be finally coming to an end, that there might be light at the end of the tunnel. I wasn't told that Betty was moving – children weren't included in conversations about major events back then – it simply trickled through. Over a few visits I started to notice packing boxes, things being moved about, clearing out going on each time. I heard snippets of conversation about 'the new house' and then eventually put it all together. It wasn't that I was stupid – far from it – no, it was just that my time at Betty's house was all focused around what her brother-in-law was doing to me. When I got there, I wondered when it would start. When it happened, I wondered when it would happen again. I was never free of the worry of it, so other things passed me by.

However, the impending move became so obvious that I couldn't miss it any longer. Betty was talking to a neighbour about their new house one day while I played with her children in the front room.

'I can't wait to get out of here,' she sighed.

'It's not that bad,' replied the other woman, indignantly, ready to take instant offence if the place she was remaining in was insulted by my auntie.

'No – well, it's just . . . we need a change,' Betty backtracked. 'And a bigger house. And I need to get away from Charlie, start over. It'll be nice to get a bit more space. I keep telling myself – this time next week and it'll all be over. I tell you, I won't be moving again in a hurry.'

Next week!

If she was moving next week, that meant that this could be the last time I ever had to put up with Eddie! I kept playing, trying to listen in and find out more, but the only thing that meant anything to me was when I heard Betty tell the woman she was talking to that it would take two buses to get to the new house. This was even better news. Eddie was lazy. I hoped that the distance and the need to get more than one bus would mean that he couldn't be bothered to visit.

That weekend Betty urged me to make sure I left nothing behind. It was official – she was moving and I'd never be back to this horrible place ever again.

On my last night with her Eddie came round with Gerry. I was happy; happy there for the first time in ages. Gerry played with me and hugged me lots. I would be sad to be away from him, but it was a price worth paying if it meant I would be out of the clutches of his disgusting brother.

As we said goodbye to them that night I was torn between sorrow at Gerry's imminent departure and glee at seeing the back of Eddie. I smiled as they said farewell – until Eddie leaned over and whispered, 'Don't worry, I'll still see you.'

'What?' I said, fear making my stomach lurch.

'I'll still come – and get you,' he smiled.

'No, no, Eddie – you can't come and see us, you can't.'

'I can do whatever I like. You'll see.'

Once Betty did move, I still visited.

'Has Eddie been round?' I would ask her, almost as soon as I got there.

'You've changed your tune,' she'd snap. 'After all those lies you told about him and now you're asking after him every second. Bloody turncoat, aren't you? Missing him, are you?'

There was no point in trying to tell her the truth; I'd tried so often in the past. I was willing to let her believe whatever she wanted as long as I was safe.

'No, he hasn't been,' she confirmed. 'Lazy bastard – he's too idle to take two buses.'

As time went on and Eddie's absence seemed to be permanent, I relaxed. He had lied. He never did come to Betty's new house, but the fear stayed with me for a long time. He was the biggest threat in my life and every visit, to begin with, was ruined because I thought he would turn up at any second.

I started to wonder whether there might be other good things coming into my life – maybe I would get to go to my mum for summer now that I was bigger? Mum was writing to me regularly, and I knew that she was married to a man called Hank and they had two little children, my half-siblings. However, I was never allowed to read her letters for myself. Granny Morag would always read them out to me and embellish every line. So, for example, when Mum would write that she missed me, Granny would scoff.

'Missing you that bloody much that she's got herself some new kids! Missing you that bloody much that she's still over there enjoying herself with her new man while I'm landed with you!'

I didn't know the truth of the matter. I didn't know whether to listen to Mum's words or give weight to what Granny was saying. There was no denying, however, that the letters gave me some comfort. As long as they came, I could convince myself that Mum was still thinking of me and wanted to stay in touch. As well as not being allowed to read them myself, I was also not allowed to reply. I knew that Granny Morag wrote back, but I had no idea of how deceitful she was being until one day when she started ranting and raving in the kitchen.

'The fucking cheek of it!' she shouted at my granddad. 'Saying that to me!'

'Well, Morag,' he replied, gently, 'you reap what you sow.'

'Oh shut up, you old fool!' she retorted.

I heard Uncle Robbie walk in and ask her what was going on.

'It's that stuck-up Yankee bastard your sister Kathleen married,' she shrieked. 'He's writing to me – insulting me!'

'What's he said? What's he said to insult you? Maybe it's not as bad as you think,' said Robbie carefully, knowing that his mother could take offence at anything.

'How can this not be a bloody insult?' she ranted. ' "We are very concerned for Sheena,"' she read, obviously quoting from a letter. ' "The notes we have received from her have shown no improvement in writing, spelling or grammar over the years. We feel that there is something lacking in her education as the letters simply do not seem to be of a suitable standard for a young girl this age. Kathleen and I would be very grateful if this could be addressed – Sheena means a great deal to both of us and if there is anything we can do to assist in her education, please let us know."'

There was silence in the room until Granny let rip again.

'The cheeky, cheeky bastard!' she shouted again. 'That's my fucking writing and spelling he's insulting!'

'You've been writing her letters?' asked Robbie.

'Of course I've been writing her letters,' said Granny.

'So, wee Sheena has been telling you what she wants to say to our Kathleen and you've written it down for her?' he continued.

'Did I raise you stupid?' Granny retorted. 'Why would I do that? *I've* been writing the letters; why would I let a wee lassie tell me what to put in them?'

'What *have* you been putting in them?' continued Robbie – I thought he was being rather brave as I could tell Granny was ready to explode.

'Whatever I fucking want!' she said. '"Everything's fine and dandy", "my granny's a wonderful woman", "don't bother coming to see me as I'm fine" – that sort of thing.'

'That sort of thing?'

'Aye, that sort of thing – the truth. That's all I write, the truth. And now I'm being insulted for my troubles! Well, those Yankee bastards will wait a long fucking time for a letter from me!' She started stomping around the kitchen, banging pots, and making as much noise as possible.

'You could just let Sheena write her own letters,' said Granddad gently.

'Are you completely mental?' came the reply. 'So she can tell her a bunch of lies? All that nonsense about Eddie – you want her wasting Kathleen's time with that? I know what I'm doing, so the best thing you can do is shut up.'

'But—'

'I said you need to shut up. So, shut up. I'm not talking about this any more.'

With that, the conversation – such as it was – concluded.

I was shocked. I knew that Granny wrote to Mum, but I had never suspected that she pretended to be me. It was a shock, but it wasn't enough to take the shine off the new happiness I felt now there was hope in my life. The fact that I was no longer around Eddie was not the only wonderful thing that happened in my life at that time. Something else magical happened. I started going to horse-riding lessons and, from that moment on, my love for horses never wavered. Their beauty and majesty has always made my heart soar, but I also discovered my own freedom when I was riding. Horses never questioned me, they never threatened me; they always gave me love and comfort. I adore all animals but horses, more than any other creature, signify so much to me as my relationship with them began at that point of my life when I did – at last – feel there was some hope.

I also adored reading. The classics, in particular, drew me in and transported me to another world. *Little Women*, *Moby Dick*, anything by Dickens – I loved them all. When I was older I discovered books by Lewis Grassic Gibbon. In *Sunset Song*, the main female character, Chris Guthrie, has her dreams thwarted by her family, and is linked to the land, living a rural life that wasn't a million miles from mine. The undercurrent of abuse she suffers also spoke to me, and when I finally read that story I felt a connection unlike any other. I love that book to this day.

Books and horses were all I had really. I didn't have friends. The kids at school bullied me and there was a real split between the types of worker on the farm – different levels just weren't supposed to mix. Not that it would have mattered really. I didn't know how to be around other children, and the only play I knew was 'dirty' play.

Auntie Betty had never believed me – or she had chosen to never do anything about what was happening publicly. Maybe she did know that I was telling the truth, maybe she knew exactly what was going on. I've always thought the way she was so keen to tell everyone what a 'liar' I was showed that she was trying to create an excuse of sorts. Any time I mentioned that Eddie was hurting me or doing things I didn't like she'd fly off the handle and announce to everyone that I told stories and could never be believed. Whatever the reality of the situation with her, I felt that her move away from Eddie was the start of a new beginning for me. There was just no reason to see him again.

I had my horse-riding and my abuser was no longer in my life.

The summer after Eddie had finally gone out of my life was a lovely one. It was hot and sunny throughout the entire school holidays, and I was outdoors from early morning until the sun disappeared at bedtime. Living near the farm meant that I had almost complete freedom. Everyone else was always busy so they didn't keep track of me. I didn't go far, but I was pretty much left to my own devices.

I was almost ten and the person closest to me in age was Granny's youngest child, Jed. He was fourteen and was known as being a bit 'simple'. I was never sure what that meant. Everyone said it and it was just accepted; in those days there was no political correctness. The words used to describe anyone who had learning difficulties were horrible and judgemental. I was never quite sure whether Morag encouraged this characterisation of him as 'slow' to stop him getting the blame for anything. Certainly if Big Kenny ever criticised him he would have to put up with his wife telling him to leave the 'boy' alone, and if anyone tried to get Jed to do his fair share of chores she would always take his side and make sure someone else stepped up to the plate.

I'm not entirely convinced there was anything 'wrong' with Jed. He was indulged, and he was his mother's favourite, that was true, and he wasn't the sharpest knife in the drawer, but I don't think there was a medical or psychological problem. She felt guilty for the childhood accident that had resulted in him having a finger amputated but that didn't affect his brain.

He worked on the farm and he brought money in, but he never had to help out as much as the rest of us. I remember playing with him a lot that summer. In retrospect I think he was the only one who was allowed time off to mess about. If Granny saw anyone else idle, she'd find something for them to do – unless they were Jed. The fact that we played together was more as a result of her allowing me to avoid some work if he was happy, rather than the other way around. He was a big lad for fourteen, and really far too old for the type of games he played with me. He would put me on his back a lot and run around with me, pretending that he was my horse. There was nothing untoward or inappropriate about it – it was just fun, genuine fun. We climbed trees together and indulged in play-fighting. We wrestled each other and raced about the farm. We were just wild kids that summer and I thought nothing of it – I thought nothing of why a fourteen-year-old was spending all of his time with a nine-year-old child.

One day, I walked into the front room and he was bending over, looking for something under the couch. I jumped onto his back – as I'd done a thousand times before – and said, 'Giddy up, horsey!'

He threw me up his back a bit higher and raced around the room with me, as usual. After a few minutes he 'galloped' through to my bedroom. As I laughed wildly, he drew himself up and threw me onto the bed.

I thought he'd had enough of the game, but I was wrong.

He had something else in mind.

It was as if he had changed in a split second, just like his mother did, just as my granny did.

As I fell on the bed my skirt flew up my legs. Before I knew what was happening Jed's hands were all over me. He was touching me in places I didn't want to be touched, places I knew I *shouldn't* be touched. I was paralysed with fear. I thought this was all over. I thought that now Eddie was out of my life, this was all finished too, so why was it happening again, why was I being touched like this again?

Jed's hands were covering me, his breath was getting faster and I knew.

I knew.

I just knew that he was going to do the same things that Eddie had done.

He was on top of me, his legs were pinning me down, either side of me. He was rubbing me all over, rubbing me in private places, and it was horrible. It would have been horrible for any child, but I couldn't believe it was happening just as it had with Eddie. What was wrong with me? Why did men want to keep doing this awful thing to me? Maybe Granny Morag was right, maybe I was nasty and they knew it.

He started to rub himself against me. Something inside me knew not to scream, knew that I would get into trouble if I drew attention to this.

'Jed,' I said quietly, with the panic rising, 'you shouldn't be doing that, it's not nice, you should stop it.'

'It's fine,' he said. 'Don't worry, just don't tell anyone. If they don't know, it's fine.'

This wasn't what I meant at all. I didn't want us to collude. I wanted him to stop.

'No, Jed,' I tried again. 'I don't want to, you need to stop.'

'It's fine, just don't tell,' he said again.

'It's not fine,' I replied. 'It's not.'

'Aye. Aye, it is. Eddie says so.'

His words chilled me to the bone. What did he mean? Why was he bringing Eddie into this? Before I knew what was happening, Jed was doing what he needed to do. Rubbing himself faster and faster against me while touching me at the same time, he brought himself to orgasm and stood up. He was still fully clothed and walked towards the door as if what had happened was the most natural thing in the world.

'Remember, Sheena – it's fine as long as no one knows,' he said, before closing the door behind him.

I stayed in my room for the rest of the day. When it was dinner and supper time, I called through that I wasn't hungry. As the darkness finally fell on that long summer night, my tears dried up and I felt able to think about what had happened.

Eddie.

He was the key to this.

Chapter 13

Home ground

I should have been safe.

At home, on my own territory, another horror was about to begin. The things Jed had done seemed to happen so quickly, but what if it wasn't out of the blue? What if he knew that those things had been done to me before? What if he knew that I had already been abused?

I remembered that Jed had spent a lot of time with Eddie. He often went poaching with him, or shooting, and they had been alone for hours on end. Had Eddie abused him too? I knew that I wasn't the only child to have suffered at his hands. I knew this because I had been there when other children were at his mercy, but it hadn't crossed my mind that Jed had been one of his victims too.

If he had, that was where the excuses came from, the plea not to tell anyone, the belief that as long as no one knew it was all right. These were things Eddie would have said to Jed as his abuser too.

It was appalling to think of. The cycle of abuse was continuing and Eddie had planted the seeds of this horror in one of his own child victims.

The next day Jed said nothing – there was no apology, no mention of what had gone on. As the long summer continued I kept away from him as much as possible but Granny Morag was watching me like a hawk.

'Have you fallen out with my Jed?' she asked one day.

I shook my head and got up to leave the room. I didn't want to have this conversation.

'I should hope not,' she said, dragging me back. 'He's not like you. That boy doesn't have a bad bone in his body, so don't you go taking advantage of him, you little madam. Do you hear me?'

I nodded my head and sat where she had shoved me. If I kept quiet, maybe she'd let this go.

'Jed!' she shouted. 'Jed! Come in here!'

I wasn't going to get out of this easily. She was like a dog with a bone sometimes.

Jed ambled in as if he had all the time and not a care in the world.

'What is it, Mum?' he asked, putting his arms around her waist and kissing her on the cheek. I could see her melt as he did so. She adored him and he had her wrapped round his little finger.

'What's going on with you and her?' She nodded towards me casually.

Jed stared at me and kept his eyes on mine as he answered, 'Nothing, nothing at all.'

'You sure?' asked Morag.

'Aye. Sure I'm sure. Why? What's she been saying? Telling stories? Making things up as usual?'

Granny Morag snorted. 'Well, she's good at that, isn't she? No, I just thought – well, you've not been playing together very much. I thought you'd had a falling out.'

Playing together.

He was fourteen years old and I was nine. The last time we had 'played together' he had sexually abused me – and my reputation as a liar and a fantasist (a reputation carefully cultivated by the woman in front of me) meant that I couldn't say a word.

'No – we're fine; aren't we, Sheena?' Jed asked pointedly.

I nodded my head in agreement – what else could I do?

'Come on then,' he said. 'Let's go play.'

'Aw, that's my boy,' beamed Granny, 'never one to hold a grudge.'

Jed came over and took my hand, leading me outside.

'See?' he said, as soon as we were clear of the house. 'I told you – as long as no one knows, as long as no one finds out, it's fine. Now, I've got to get this tree chopped down. You sit there while I'm busy.'

I did as I was told – like always – and sat making daisy chains while Jed got on with things. I thought that if I could just keep out of his way, keep as invisible as possible, things would be fine. If it meant that we couldn't mess around together that was a small price to pay. I couldn't bear the thought that he could turn into a beast like Eddie, and I prayed that nothing else would happen. It was a warm day and I was tired. I hadn't slept well since the day of Jed touching me, and I dozed off as I lay on the grass. I don't know how long I was asleep, but I woke up with a strange feeling that someone was watching me. As I blinked my eyes open against the fierce midday sun I saw Jed propped up on his elbows at my side.

'What are you doing?' I snapped.

'Nothing. Just watching you. Nothing,' he replied defensively.

'It must be nearly lunchtime,' I said, trying to distract him with the idea of food, which was usually his main concern. 'Let's go in before we get shouted at.'

'It's fine,' he replied casually. 'She doesn't shout at me.'

He was right. He was the golden boy, no matter what.

'I'll go back to sleep then,' I told him. I didn't mean it – there was no way I would risk lying there unguarded while he was so close to me – but I hoped that he would think it sounded very dull and he'd leave me alone to get on with his tree chopping.

I was out of luck.

'I'll just lie here too then,' said Jed.

I closed my eyes partially – enough to make him think I was asleep and very boring, hopefully, but not enough that I couldn't see if he made a move towards me. I must have stayed like that for half an hour but, eventually, the heat got the better of me and I started to feel myself dropping off again. Before I knew it, his lips were on mine. He was pushing into me, trying to prise my mouth open with his tongue, attempting to really, properly kiss me.

In spite of everything that had been done to me, this felt like an appalling invasion. I didn't want to be kissed like that. I didn't want to respond and I wouldn't, no matter what. Jed was getting more and more agitated, but I kept my lips pressed tight against each other. I tried to push him away but he was much stronger. I was scared to shout out in any way as that would mean I'd have to open my mouth and the thought of his tongue in there made me want to vomit.

I was aghast that he would be trying to do this. In fact I couldn't even understand why he would be trying to put his tongue in there in the first place. We didn't have television, I'd never seen such a thing – where did he get this horrible idea from, I wondered.

Finally, he gave up and rolled away.

'Don't you ever do that again!' I shouted, not caring whether anyone would hear me. 'That's dirty! It's so, so dirty!'

To me it was dirty. I'd been touched before, I'd been raped – that had become almost the norm with Eddie, but this ... this *kissing*? It was dirty; it was horribly dirty. Eddie had never, ever tried to kiss me, thank God, so this really horrified me.

Jed looked at me as if he couldn't quite understand what was going on. Perhaps he wondered why I was causing such a commotion over a kiss if he had got away with rubbing himself on me and touching me so much that he ejaculated. The thing was, when he had touched me a few days earlier I had known by the look on his face that this is what he wanted from me. I felt as if I had a sign on me that said 'Do what you want – I'm here for anybody'. But kissing? That wasn't part of the deal, not in my mind.

Jed sighed as if he was very confused by the whole business.

'Well – do you want to play horsey then? You like that, don't you, because you like horses?'

It was exactly what Eddie used to say to me. After he'd abused me, he would always chat about horses, get me to help him with his betting choices and talk about the horse he would buy me on a day that would never come. This all fitted in with what Jed had said to me that first time; now I was sure that they had spoken about me, that Eddie had told him he could do whatever he wanted and that I would keep quiet. It felt like déjà vu – and I could do nothing about it.

From that point on Jed wanted to play 'horsey' all the time. He was cunning with it, completely wrecking his mother's arguments that he was simple or too stupid to be sly. He would wait until Granny Morag was there before throwing me on his back, or saying that he was going to play with me. She would glow with pride at what a good boy he was, and usually make some comments about how I didn't deserve such a lovely uncle who always made time for me. He would do a bit of running around in front of everyone else before heading off to either his bedroom or mine. He'd throw me down and then start touching me. The thing was, if he was so simple how would he know to keep it all secret? He was the one who said it was all fine as long as no one knew about it, and he was the one who kept up the pretence of us playing. The fact that he always did things when no one was looking and he always told me to keep quiet proves to me that he knew exactly what he was up to – and that he had learned at the feet of a master. Of course, it is appalling if he was also abused by Eddie but that isn't an excuse.

Many people say that abusers tend to have been abused

themselves and that may very well be the case, but it is a huge slap in the face to any survivor who has made a life for themselves, despite what was done to them and having never laid a finger on their own children, to say that they are trapped in a cycle of abuse. Everyone can break out of it. Jed made his choices whereas I had none.

Another sad part of this was that, because I was still so young, I did desperately want to play with someone. I didn't really have any friends and the only person who would play with me was taking it too far. He didn't touch me every time, which was how he drew me in. Each time I thought it might really just be playing but then, every so often, it would go to that horrible other level. I never knew which version of playing it would be – the happy, fun, clean one, or the twisted Jed game.

I said nothing to Granny Morag because I knew she wouldn't believe me. She must have suspected something, because of her reaction pretty much every time I opened my mouth. Granny called me a 'wee bastard' and she used the word 'cunt' a lot. It was just how she spoke to me when in a temper and, even as I write this, I know that I'm not being entirely accurate with her words because if I actually wrote them down as she spoke, you'd have nothing to read but a stream of swearing every time I told a story.

It was as if she had a split personality. The truth is she did take me in. She did look after me all those years. She did it badly – but she did it nonetheless. But when she changed, when she became the angry, nasty woman who thought the abuse in my life was nothing, she swore even more. I got the brunt. I got the worst of it. There were things which she would say over and over again to me:

You lying wee bastard.

You evil wee cunt.

Don't you tell your lies, you wee bitch.

Don't you stand there sinning your bastard soul with your fucking lies.

Don't tell fucking stories — don't run my Jed down, you wee whore.

You should think black burning shame of yourself for the lies you fucking tell about poor Jed.

That was her favourite. She was always telling me I should 'think black burning shame' of myself. For everything. The odd thing was, even when I didn't mention Jed's name, she'd assume I was going to say he'd done something. If I came in hungry and started to say, 'Granny, can I . . .?' she'd scream, 'No, you fucking CANNOT tell me something about poor Jed! You leave that poor laddie alone, him with all his problems, him never being able to find a lassie to love him! You should think black burning shame of yourself for telling such lies!' All I was going to ask her for was something to eat but she had a guilty conscience on his behalf. She always thought I was about to tell her about something awful he'd done or tried to do. She knew more than she let on — and she knew that he wasn't the saint she made him out to be.

Chapter 14

Giving up

The 'horseplay' had been going on for about three months when things changed. I was back at school by that point, and the nights were getting longer as autumn moved into winter. I had turned ten. My bedroom was my sanctuary. No one really bothered me when I was in there. I would get called out if there were chores to be done but I was largely left alone as it was assumed – rightly – that I was reading. This was something Granny Morag approved of. She was a woman of contradictions and while she seemed to despise me for most of the time she also showed pride in me when telling others about my love of books. In fact, she took it one stage further by making up stories about my intellectual capabilities which couldn't possibly be true. I remember her telling people that I had been able to read while I was in my pram, before I could walk, which was obviously impossible but no one liked to contradict Granny Morag with cold, hard facts!

My bedroom was my own place. In a house which only had boys left in it – apart from Granny, of course – it was also the only place where I could get some privacy. While they all had to share, I was given a room to myself. In some ways this was odd because, after all, it wasn't as if any heed had been paid to keeping me safe in other ways, but no matter the reasoning behind it I was grateful. I hadn't always been alone in that room but by now all of the other girls had left, and I was the only one in it. It was a big room and it had a recess for the bed. If anyone passed the door they couldn't see me on the bed. There was a couch in front of the coal fire but I rarely read there, I preferred the bed.

One Saturday night I was lying on top of my bedclothes, reading as always. I had cleaned the kitchen, peeled the potatoes, taken scraps out to the pigs and done the dozen other chores expected of me that day. Before bedtime I had banked the fires down, cleaned the dishes, laid out the breakfast things for the next morning and given everywhere a sweep. It had been a busy day. If there was anything else to do, even at this late hour, I knew I'd hear my name shrieked soon enough but, for the moment, I was free. I was wrapped up in a fantasy world for hours. I didn't even know if everyone else had gone to bed because the story had pulled me in and that was all I cared about. I always read for hours, until my eyes couldn't stay open any longer, and that night was no different. I don't know what time it was but I woke with a start, the bedroom dark, the book lying at my side – and Jed's fingers inside me.

I hadn't heard him come in, I hadn't even heard the door opening, but he was there. He was poking me, horribly and painfully. My first instinct was actually that Eddie had broken into the house. This felt like exactly the same thing he did to me, the same horrible agonising touching. Could that have happened? For a moment I thought it could. He knew where I lived, and I still thought it was a miracle that he hadn't come for me. However, his smell wasn't there and soon I heard Jed's voice saying, 'Just be quiet, Sheena, it's fine – just be quiet.'

I didn't scream. I would have woken the whole house at that time of night and I knew what would happen. Jed would disappear before anyone got there, Granny would just shout at me from her room, or the whole family would arrive at my bedside, giving me dog's abuse for nothing. If Jed had been found there, I was sure that I would get the blame. He would act daft and concoct some story that would leave me looking bad.

Screaming wasn't an option. I was in this alone.

I was squirming about, trying to escape from him.

'Lie still!' he whispered harshly. 'And open your legs!'

'No, Jed! No!' I said.

I had been asleep on my side and he was at the back of me with his hand in front. He was getting himself all worked up and suddenly I was aware that he was pushing his erection into the back of me. I couldn't bear to go through what Eddie had done to me in the toilets.

When Jed pulled me over and entered me from the front, I was almost relieved. God knows, Eddie had done that plenty of times. Writing this, I am faced with the full horror of it all again. I was ten years old and I was relieved, *relieved*, that I was being raped vaginally because I knew the pain I would suffer for days on end if it was done elsewhere. How sick is that? My world was so warped and so ruined by the things done to me by Eddie that

I had already thought through the uselessness of screaming, realised it wouldn't make any difference, and accepted my fate. I was glad of the lesser of two evils. It's horrendous looking back, but it's what my life was.

That was the start of it.

After that it was every time he could get his hands on me.

When Jed left that night – as soon as he had done what he wanted – he warned me to keep quiet. There was none of the softly, softly approach of earlier. He wasn't implying there was nothing wrong with this, simply that I had to make sure no one found out. He knew what he was doing and how wrong it was.

'You better not breathe a word of this to anyone,' he hissed. 'You shut your mouth – understand? You shut it, and you keep it shut.'

That was it. I lived in the same house as my abuser. We had been raised as brother and sister. I had never called him 'Uncle' and his mother had taken the place of my mother. It was a warped, perverted set-up and I was stuck in it without hope of escape.

I think that was the night I stopped believing Mummy would come for me. This was my life and if she had wanted me she would have come by now. That hurt more than anything Eddie or Jed had ever done to me. Physical pain passes, emotional scars stay for ever. Even though she didn't know what was happening to me, I still couldn't understand why she could leave me here, especially now that it seemed like for ever. The very life that she had been so desperate to escape from was what I was sentenced to. By going she had made sure that her little girl, her firstborn, was left in the house, in the world that she herself had hated. If Mum had stayed with us this wouldn't have happened. If she had come back for me this wouldn't have happened. I know now that the abuse was entirely the fault of my abusers but, as a little girl desperate for her mummy, it seemed to me that she was the key to everything. She still wrote, she still sent me beautiful clothes, she still parcelled up lovely gifts of toys and books, but I didn't want any of that. I wanted *her* and I wanted away from this.

As I lay there, bleeding again from yet another man's cruel treatment, I wept. I thought of all the stories she had told me of America. She had said she was going there to make a life for *us*, but she had only made a life for herself. She had married, she had given birth to other babies, and she had forgotten about the child she had back in Scotland. It was easy to send letters and dresses; it wasn't easy to be the one waiting.

From the next day onwards Jed got to me whenever he could. When I tried to stop him, when I made it clear that this was not what I wanted, he started to say to me, 'If you tell you'll go to jail.'

This was just what Eddie used to say. When I was little I believed it. He had told me that if anyone knew what he was doing to me, they would know I was bad and they would send me away. When Betty and Granny began to tell everyone that I was a liar and a fantasist, Eddie's threat was compounded. It made sense. If I was the bad one, if I was the liar, then the police would be very cross with me. They liked good little girls who did as they were told. The threat of jail had all but silenced me with Eddie and it did the same with Jed. It was, of course, another clue that he had been abused by Eddie himself — I could now assume that the threat used to keep me quiet had also been used against him. Jed had learned through bitter experience just how effective it was and he was employing it now that he had turned abuser. I also wondered, in later years, how much of my abuse had been discussed between Eddie and Jed, but I would never know. Had Jed been told that this was a way he could keep me in line? I have no idea, but it worked. Even at ten years old, I thought I was bad and I thought I could be sent to prison.

Although Jed was still at school, he worked on the farm at weekends and in his spare time. With his older brother, Robbie, they did enough labour to ensure that we kept the linked cottage we all lived in. It came with the job, and this soon became another way to threaten me. If I ever did get some strength to say that I would tell, and if I ever did act as if going to jail was not an issue for me, Jed would use a different angle.

'What if someone thinks I've done something wrong?' he would ask me, as if the very idea was ridiculous. 'What if I get sent to jail even though I've done nothing bad? We'd lose the house. We'd all get kicked out if I wasn't here to work as well. It would be your fault, Sheena. We'd all be homeless and it would be your fault.'

He did actually have a good argument there. The linked cottage would be lost if there weren't enough men to work the land and ensure that we could remain housed. So this became the price I paid. Jed did whatever he wanted to me, whenever he wanted, and I was left with the threat that, if I told, I would be jailed or we would lose the house. It was such a clever and cunning way to keep me in line that it completely wrecks the argument of anyone who would claim that Jed didn't know what he was doing. He knew exactly what he was doing, and he knew just how to keep me quiet.

Just before Christmas that year, when I had turned ten a couple of months earlier, Jed was allowed to leave school. The leaving age was younger in those days and if there was a job to go to for someone who had absolutely no academic inclinations, no one stood in their way. This meant that Jed did become the main breadwinner (again, quite a feat for someone whose mother said he was incapable of anything), and the house was tied to his labour. Robbie and the other laddies moved off the land and got jobs elsewhere, leaving Jed the only one to keep a roof over our heads.

Jed couldn't read or write – but that could have just been bad education or undiagnosed dyslexia. If any strangers came round, he would shut himself in another room and refuse to speak with them, Granny always said he was unable to talk to strangers, but that could have been shyness or social ineptitude rather than selective mutism. She was always looking for a reason for him to be the way he was. He certainly wasn't clever, not in a book-reading sense, but he had an intelligence that allowed him to carry out his perversions unnoticed which belied any daftness she labelled him with.

He was always looking for me. He raped me once a day for years. Once he started it was consistent but it took me a while to realise that, unlike Eddie, he wouldn't really vary what he did. He found his favourite things, his favourite places, and he stuck with them.

What I remember about Jed tends to be focused on one thing. When I think about it I feel as if I've been transported back. Every sense I possess flies back to that one place and I feel the dread of it as if it's happening all over again.

Jed raced pigeons.

I hated them. They were dirty, smelly, noisy creatures and I kept away from where he kept them as much as possible. I suppose it was only a matter of time before he put the two things together – his love of abusing me and his love of pigeons.

I never liked to go into the pigeon loft and would always try to avoid it. One day, Granny Morag said to me, 'Here, take these sandwiches out to Jed.'

'Where is he?' I asked. He could be anywhere on the farm or the wider estate. I wasn't too scared of going to him if I had something like this to do – I was scared of Granny's reaction if I refused. I didn't think he'd do anything in broad daylight when other people could catch him.

'He's in the pigeon loft,' she told me. 'He's been there all morning, looking after them. He loves those birds – he's a good laddie.'

I ignored that last bit.

'I'm sure he'll be in soon,' I said, trying to avoid going to the loft. 'He can just have his food when he comes in.'

'No,' said Granny firmly. 'He loses all track of time out there. Do as you're told, and take him his sandwiches.'

There was no point arguing with her. I took the wrapped sandwiches and left. When I got to the door of the pigeon loft, I threw them down on the ground and shouted, 'Jed! There's your food!'

I'd planned to run away but he was standing just behind the door. Instead of shouting out in reply to me, he simply stepped out into the light and grabbed my wrist.

'That's not very nice,' he said. 'Throwing my grub down like that. I bet you were told to give it to me, weren't you?'

I nodded.

'I thought you'd be busy,' I said weakly.

'Well, you're in luck. I'm not,' he replied. 'Come in here.'

I looked at the sandwiches lying on the ground and acted daft. 'No, Jed – you don't want to have your lunch in there. It stinks. Come and sit outside.' I felt safer outside. I didn't want to go into that horrible place.

'Are you stupid? It's freezing. Anyway, I'm not hungry. Get in here.'

He was still holding me by the wrist and I tried to pull away, squirming from his firm grip. I kept saying 'No' but it made no difference. He dragged me in and threw me down on the floor. I tried to get up, but, again, it was no use. He was so much stronger and we both knew what he was planning. He always preferred to take me from behind, so I panicked whenever I was in that position. I tried to twist round but he was on me quickly and heavily.

The whole place was filthy. There was pigeon shit everywhere. They were sitting on perches all around and above, fouling the loft constantly. He didn't really keep it clean, despite Granny saying how wonderful he was with the birds. I was on my knees in the stinking shit of that disgusting loft, with the smell of those horrible birds in my nose, wanting to gag as they cooed around me. I hated pigeons. I'll always hate pigeons.

There were hundreds of them in three huge sections. They were all racing pigeons and he loved them dearly. I'm sure it was perfect for him to do those things to me there as it was his favourite place. There was nothing for me to distract myself with; I would usually try to focus on looking at something or smelling something or listening to something, or even imagining things if all else failed, but I was surrounded by pigeons. Their smell and sound and mess were everywhere. They were all I could hear. They were all I could see. They were all I could smell. Even when I tried to send my mind elsewhere their presence was so overpowering it couldn't be done.

When he was finished, I got up and ran away as fast as I could. I belted through the door of the cottage, where Granny was still in the kitchen.

'Did you see Jed?' she shouted. 'Did you see Jed?'

Yes, I wanted to scream, I saw Jed and he'll be in my nightmares again tonight.

Chapter 15

Obsession

Jed's obsession with the pigeons continued and I swear that he knew how much I hated that loft as he tried to get me there constantly. He was becoming as obsessed with me and what he could do to me as he was with those birds.

One day I went into the kitchen for some breakfast. He was already there talking to his mum.

'Here,' she said to me. 'Jed's got an idea. He's not too good with his letters . . .' – this was true as he couldn't write a word – 'so you can help him with something.'

'What?' I asked, immediately suspicious about what they had cooked up together.

'He needs to log the pigeon numbers,' replied Granny.

'He can do that himself,' I cried.

'No, he cannot, you know he can't write well – don't you go making him feel bad about it.'

I did know that he couldn't write well, he couldn't write at all actually, but I also knew that he had developed his own system. Each pigeon had a metal ring on its leg with a personal number and I knew that Jed simply memorised each individual bird, even though there were hundreds of them. I tried to explain this to Granny but she was having none of it.

'Don't talk rubbish,' she said. 'You're bone bloody idle and you're just trying to get out of it.'

I was, but not for the reasons she thought.

'I don't want to,' I said, in a rare show of defiance. 'He can manage.'

'You'll do as you're told! Christ, I work my fingers to the bones for you, you lazy bitch; the least you can do is read the numbers and write them down.'

I knew what he was up to. It was just a ploy to get me in that horrible pigeon loft with a legitimate excuse.

'I'm not touching them,' I muttered.

'I'll do that,' said Jed.

'And it'll be quick,' I continued. 'I'll get it done really quickly.'

'No – it'll take ages,' said Jed. 'It needs to be done properly.'

'I'll do it with Robbie,' I countered. 'He could read the numbers to me and I'll write them down!'

'No, Robbie doesn't like the pigeons,' Jed reminded Morag.

'Neither do I!' I said.

'You're just a lazy bugger,' said Granny. 'You'll do this. You'll go to that loft and you'll do whatever Jed says. You'll take as long as he needs and you'll feel the back of my hand if you complain.'

So, that was it. Jed – poor, simple Jed who everyone said couldn't hold an idea in his head – had concocted a foolproof plan to have me alone in a place I hated, whenever he wanted.

The pattern began. He would always find something to do with the pigeons which needed my help in the loft. It was writing their numbers down, or making a list of their names, or counting how many there were of each colour. The irony was that if we had actually been doing those things, it wouldn't have taken long at all; it was the fact that the imagined tasks were never done because he spent the time abusing me which allowed him to claim they were unfinished.

There would be times when he made a pretence of actually logging them. When we went into the loft, he would pick up one of those disgusting, stinking birds and hold out its leg. I'd read the number out loud and he would say, 'Write it down.' I don't know what this charade was for. If he was really as incapable of reading and writing as he seemed to be, I could have been saying anything. I've often wondered whether he could do more than he admitted and whether he was, in fact, checking up on me. He would then tell me the colour of the bird – even though I could see it perfectly well for myself – and I'd write that beside the number. Jed would then tell me its name, which I would also write down. Sometimes he would bring out a new notebook or piece of paper. When I'd ask him where the other figures were, he'd just say that he'd lost it and we'd have to start all over again.

On some days he would start touching me as soon as we went into the loft. On other days he would wait until the pigeon logging was underway. Just as I had ended up grateful that he was raping me vaginally rather than anally, I used to pray for the days when he would get on with the abuse, as I simply couldn't bear waiting in that horrible place with those loathsome creatures. I knew that he would always abuse me – there was never, ever an occasion when he didn't if we were in there; my only hope was that it would be quick. The pigeons all sat on little pegs above me while it was happening – they all had individual pegs to perch on – and it seemed as if all they did was shit. As I was being abused, I would get covered in it, on my hair, on my face, everywhere. Those birds needed to be fed and watered daily, so Jed always had a reason to be there, and he always seemed to find a reason for me to be there too.

He continued to prefer to enter me from behind. I don't know whether this was to prevent him seeing my face or prevent me seeing his. On the few times when I did see him during his attacks on me, his face was the stuff of nightmares. He was ugly enough at the best of times, but during this his face would be contorted and he would drool with excitement. I'm sure he didn't prefer that angle out of any thought for me, but I was glad that I couldn't see him, and that he couldn't see the shame and agony on my own face either.

After this had been going on for about a year I had to face up to another horrible issue. I believed that Granny Morag knew what was going on and was turning a blind eye to it. She often spoke of how Jed 'needed a lassie', of how he would never get a wife because he was so 'simple'. She wasn't stupid. I'm quite sure that if I had been disappearing with another boy for so long, so often, she would have had something to say about it. Given that she was so on top of knowing what I was doing for most of the time if I was around the farm, it seems odd that she would let me disappear for ages on end with Jed.

It was a busy life. I had lots of chores to do. Granddad spent all of his day splitting logs and sawing them into sticks. When I got in from school my job was to sort the sticks into bags for us and others, and to pack them into boxes. Jed had to help out with milking as well as other jobs around the farm. During the summer months he would take me into the pigeon loft once the chores were done but, during winter, when it got dark much earlier, he would abuse me in my room a lot of the time. His favourite excuse then was to get me to read his pigeon books and magazines to him. He always said that needed to be done in my bedroom as we needed peace and quiet. Granny Morag would collude with this. If I tried to resist he would shout, 'Mother! Get her told! She won't read my pigeon books to me!'

Granny would then make excuses for him as always.

'You ungrateful wee bitch,' she'd shriek at me. 'You know that laddie's got no pleasures in his life, yet you'd deny him this? Do you think he wants to be dependent on you? Don't be so bloody horrible – get through to that room and read to him.'

There was no reading going on. He'd grin at me each time it happened. Tuesday was the worst day. That was when Granny bought him that week's edition of the *Pigeon Gazette* and when she expected us to take much more time in my bedroom as I 'read' to him.

There were times when I tried to open up a conversation with her about what her son was doing to me, but it was hopeless. She hated me and she adored him. I was still hearing what I had always heard – that my mother had abandoned me, that I was unlovable, that I should be grateful that I had been looked after by my selfless grandmother. She added to this that Jed was simple, he needed a woman, he would never have a normal relationship. How much of that was code, I wonder now? Was she actually telling me that the price I had to pay for a roof over my head all those years was to fill the role of an uncomplaining 'woman' and sexual partner for my own uncle.

I didn't make friends at school because of what Jed was doing to me, and what Eddie had done before him. Abuse doesn't just affect a child while it's happening. It touches every part of your life during and after. It's hard to describe to anyone who hasn't been through it, but I'll bet every penny I have that there will be plenty of people reading this who know *exactly* what I mean. When you're abused (and even before you know what 'abuse' is — you might think of it as pain, or hurting, or bad touching, or a million other things, but you *know* you don't want it) a light goes out. You don't live — you survive.

Even when the abuse isn't happening, you wonder when it will happen again. I was always sore. I hurt when I went to the toilet. I hurt when I sat down. I hurt when I walked. I hurt when I lay in my bed at night. I was always scared. My stomach was in knots — it churned — and I was on edge all the time. I could never relax because, even when I wasn't near Jed, the knowledge of what he did, and what he was continuing to do, was there constantly.

It was as if he was stalking me without even having to be there. He was a ghost in my life and a sense of him was always around. A child who is being abused never plays freely, never laughs without wondering when the laughter will stop, never feels that they are entitled to what should be every child's right. There is no sense of safety because everything that should make your world right, is wrong.

In my world, it was happening in the very place where I should have been safe. My uncle was my abuser and my grandmother was facilitating it. The woman who had taken my mother from me and made sure she could never get me back, was betraying me, still further, every single day of my life.

I didn't want people to be near me. I was scared to take them home, and I was worried they'd find out. I knew there was something different about me. I started to think it was my fault. It hadn't just happened with Eddie – it had happened with Jed too. What was there about me? What was wrong with me? Did I send off a signal? Did these men think that it was fine to do these things to me? If so – why? Why did I matter so little?

I tried to reason it out and I kept coming to the same conclusion. I was dirty. I was evil. I was bad.

Granny had a reputation for being a witch. The customs and folklore of rural Scotland back then meant that this was a lot easier to believe than if we'd been staying in a modern house in the city. Every farming family was linked to the land. We knew things about the seasons and the beasts, the weather and what was coming – cunning ways that couldn't be learned from books; it was just in your blood. Granny could predict things – whether any of that was magic or whether she was just a canny old woman who'd lived on her wits for so long was debatable, but I learned much of it too. She didn't teach me as such. I just looked and learned.

She kept a black candle on the mantelpiece in our kitchen and if anyone got on the wrong side of her she would light it and curse them. When I was about twelve I started to make the same threats. I would cling on to anything that might give me even a chance of protection, and if pretending to be a witch would help then I'd try that.

Stories were told about my family having witch blood running through its veins. We were supposedly descended from the East Lothian witches around the Dunbar area, many of whom had been burned at the stake or drowned in the ducking ponds. These stories were a great source of embarrassment to a lot of the outer family, such as Granny's sisters who wanted nothing to do with such tales, as they were 'church' folk.

One thing Granny did teach me was 'reading the fire', and she also passed on a lot of knowledge about natural medicine. We'd walk for miles in the springtime, and she'd describe everything, letting me eat the young leaves of certain trees, like the hawthorn, which was meant to be a tonic. Later on she'd get me to chew clover, both red and white, and tell me which plants were good and which to avoid, and the medicinal properties of them all. She could be an amazing person when she was in her right mind.

Her family, who was said to have the second sight, hailed originally from Aberdeenshire. These were the stories I loved, and I was always pestering her to tell me more – I was happy at those times. She told me that her grandfather was always talking to the dead. He would walk to the bothy at the farm where he worked and tell tales of being accompanied by the Hairy Man of the Woods. This apparition appeared beside him after he was attacked by travelling folk who stole his cigarettes and lighter. He said that as he approached the bridge crossing each time after he was robbed, the Hairy Man would walk out from the trees and saunter alongside him till he reached the farm safely.

Morag and her siblings had their interest piqued by the stories to the extent that they followed their grandfather one night. When they saw the Hairy Man, they ran for their lives! It's a place I know well and when I walk there I never feel scared or spooked – I've often wondered if something or someone is walking beside me.

The old man was famed for predicting his own death, saying he would fall from a great height and meet his maker within a few weeks of the stories beginning. Amazingly, it transpired that he did indeed fall from a high barn roof, and died three weeks after that accident.

When I was a little girl I would try to persuade Granny Morag to tell me these stories whenever I could. I don't know whether I was drawn to that side of our history anyway or whether I saw it as a way to make her more like the granny I loved; whatever the reason, I sought out any folklore and magic tales during those hard times.

There was a wee cottage about two miles from us. It was an idyllic place beside a burn. The woman living there was called Jessie McClue and she would tell your fortune if you crossed her hand with silver. The other women in the village hated her and I could never understand why. All I knew was that they said she only ever told the fortune of men who went to see her and they all had a good cackle when they repeated what she told them:

'You'll be smiling when you leave my door.' It meant nothing to me but she was a bit of an enigma in my eyes because she was so unlike the other women around me. Although she had no man to support her, she always had money and even a car. She had lots of soldiers visiting to have their 'fortunes' told, and enough cash to send her son to boarding school.

I didn't understand the rumours and just focused on the fact that she was another woman who was meant to have powers. Jessie was kind to me and would make me a cup of tea with a slice of cake. She loved animals too, and as my obsession with horses and other creatures developed Jessie was a kindred spirit, always willing to talk about the natural world and share stories.

There was also an old woman called Tilly who lived in one of the cottages nearby. She was completely mad and everyone spoke about her – but they kept their distance too and never made fun of her to her face.

One of the things Tilly did was to sit on her own hens' eggs, trying to hatch them. She'd sit there for hours, day after day, looking completely confused about the fact that she'd get up with a wet arse one day and then go back the next day to a broken pile of shells, completely forgetting that she had broken them in the first place!

Old Tilly used to tell me stories about witches and the power of women while she sat on the eggs. I'd listen to her for hours, focusing on her tales rather than thinking about what she was actually doing. One day she got off the eggs long enough to go for a walk with me. We walked for miles and ended up at a house which had belonged to the local blacksmith many, many years ago.

'His sister was a witch, you know,' said Tilly. 'And he was . . . well, he was something dark as well, God knows what. Do you know about them?' she asked. 'Do you know about the Old Ones, Sheena?' That was the name given to anyone who had skills or talents in the past; anyone who had been called a witch; anyone who had scared or helped the community with their ways.

She rabbited on about all of this for a while and I was fascinated. I was drawn to the idea that I could take some power and change what was happening to me. Granny Morag had always made people think she had old ways; it would be wonderful if some of that was passed on to me or if I could make people *think* it was the case.

I held on to one thing in particular that Tilly said: 'If *someone* was bad, the Old Ones would help you; the Old Ones would never let bad go unpunished if an innocent had been hurt.'

I hardly said a word to Tilly. The stories were buzzing round my head and I was desperate to take in everything she said. To me, at that moment, she seemed very different to the mad old woman who would chase people with a broom. When she was angry she would take up a brush and try to whack the local kids with it if they annoyed her, or she'd throw stones at them. I didn't see her that way now – she was a woman with a link to the past and the potential to help me access something which might keep me safe.

We became friends that day. I loved stories anyway but the things she said about the past sparked something off for me. It was my link to something bigger. I had read so many fantasy tales and was obsessed by *The Lord of the Rings* at that point, so was obviously a prime candidate for anything mystical, but there was something inside me which said *I'm going to be a witch because then nobody can hurt me*.

I spent a lot of time with Tilly after that. When she realised that I was interested in and drawn to her stories, she revealed even more. She said that there had been witches in my past and that some of the women in my family tree had been burned at the stake during Scotland's notorious witch-hunts. The history was there and Tilly knew everything. She also knew the back stories in our community and she passed them all on to me. I had no idea of the amount of inbreeding and abuse all around me until Tilly opened my eyes. By the end of that summer I knew so many secrets, which brother was sleeping with which sister, which father hopped between the beds of all his daughters, who was really the biological dad of every child for miles around. Tilly was a fount of knowledge – but she gave me more than gossip, she gave me hope. If I could access the sort of things she was talking about, if I could draw on the powers of the Old Ones, then I could maybe, just maybe, break away from what Jed was doing to me and from what, it now seemed, was happening in practically every household around.

I did wonder whether to tell Tilly what was happening to me but she had such a loose tongue that I didn't really trust her to keep it to herself. If it had got out, with her as the source, then I doubt if anyone would have believed it – she was thought of as a daft old woman, someone to be ridiculed, and while I believed every word she said I didn't think anyone would believe my story if it came through her. I also didn't want her to think that I was bad. I believed what everyone said about me being dirty and a liar. Even when I knew in my heart of hearts that it wasn't true, the words hit home and I felt that was my identity. I was a bad girl. I was a dirty girl. I was a girl whose mother had run away to the other side of the world rather than be with her. If I told Tilly that I was also a girl who was being forced into sex by her uncle, I wasn't sure that she would see me as anything other than that bad, dirty girl and I couldn't risk it because I was getting so much from the friendship with this strange old woman.

I hung on to every word she uttered.

When she had her moments of clarity it was as if the world finally made sense. When she told me about the old blacksmith and his sister I began to join things up. From what she said they had an incestuous relationship and lived together as husband and wife. I began to think that the whole world I lived in was riddled with such things, but I also began to read everything I could about witches.

Every time my granny put a curse on someone I listened to what she said and I watched to see if it came true. I probably fitted a lot of the 'facts' to suit myself, but I got some strength from it too. I began to think that there was something in me that was old and potent; and I started to threaten Jed as often as I could bring myself to challenge his own brand of male power.

There was a library nearby and I could go there by myself. Granny never bothered about me if I left first thing in the morning and spent all day there, reading books. I accessed every book they had on witchcraft, every story, every factual book, every bit of history – I soaked it all up. The librarians got to know me and they allowed me access to the restricted sections in which there were really old texts about the witch trials and about the impact the search for witches had on the local community centuries earlier.

I felt a link to those women – and it gave me hope.

Chapter 16

Unchanging

The myths around Jed continued. Granny Morag would thump me if she saw him hanging around. If he was bothering me, or trying to touch me, I was the one she would hit. Once, when I was about ten, I tried to tell her that he was doing bad things to me and I hated it.

'After all I've done for you!' she said – one of her lines which she repeated ad nauseam. 'You should be bloody grateful that I've given you a home all these years, instead you repay me by telling lies about our poor Jed.'

That was always the line – poor Jed didn't know what he was doing. Poor Jed was simple.

Everything was always about protecting him and if I tried to stop it or say anything I was punished by her. Jed just wanted me in the pigeon loft all the time. It went on for years. Jed never sodomised me; he just wanted sex. I would say it wasn't as bad but that just shows what had been done to me by Eddie. Of course it was bad, but it didn't seem *as* bad. I was older. I went along with it. I was trained. I'd been there.

I was abused so many times that I lost my self-worth. You don't even see yourself as a person any more. You're just bad-ness, and badness will follow you. I was constantly told that if I didn't accept the abuse, something bad would happen, and I just absorbed that. I was trying to save everyone else and I do that to this day. I was told others would go to jail or we'd lose the house or I'd see other kids being lined up to be abused, and I'd think *I can fix that*. And there was only one way to do it, so that's what I did. Abusers sniff that a mile away.

Jed would say, 'Think yourself lucky I'm not sticking it in your mouth,' and I'd wonder whether Eddie had done that to him or whether they'd discussed what had been done to me. Accord-ing to Morag he didn't know anything, he was a poor soul. Yet if he was that bad he wouldn't know right from wrong, he wouldn't have kept it under wraps, or managed to hide abusing his niece for years. It was all a lie, a front to keep him safe and me a victim.

Around me the family was changing. Granddad had died. Some of the others had left home. Rose, the one who I was clos-est to, had been sent to the nuns as she was pregnant out of wedlock. There was a pattern there that no one seemed keen to break, not even her own mother who had been so horribly pun-ished during her first two pregnancies.

Just as Jed was Granny's favourite son, Nellie was her favourite daughter. Rose would be punished severely for things that would make Morag laugh when Nellie did them. I went to see Rose one day with Granny. The home for young pregnant women was close to Edinburgh Zoo. As we walked in we were faced with a huge winding staircase. On their knees were dozens of young girls, all pregnant, all scrubbing the floor and the steps.

It was like something out of a Victorian melodrama. There were nuns all around them, watching, keeping them quiet. When Rose saw us, she struggled to her feet. Her belly was huge by then and her eyes were red from crying.

'Take me home, please take me home,' she pleaded.

Granny Morag stood there impassively.

'You made your bed; you'll fucking lie in it,' she replied. She grabbed my hand and we walked off. We didn't even take our coats off and went straight home, a four-hour round trip just so that she could say that to her youngest daughter. I don't think I've ever felt so sorry for anyone as I felt for Rose that day.

On the way back Granny Morag started ranting.

'What have I done to deserve all of this?' she said. 'First your mother, then this one. Selfish bitches. Dirty whores. Your mother only ever thought of herself; she didn't care about you, she just wanted a new life, she thought she was better than anyone else. And that one back there? If she thinks I'm going to raise her bastard like I raised you, she's got another think coming.'

Rose's baby was taken away from her when she was born and given up for adoption. After that Rose came back, but she was changed. She was terrified of her mother – and of Nellie, her older sister. Nellie was a bully. She was like my granny and would just laugh if she saw me trying to get away from Jed.

If I had any suspicions that Granny knew what was going on I was left in no doubt not long after my thirteenth birthday. Jed had been abusing me for well over three years and the pattern remained the same. There was little variety in what he did – it was just the usual bad things over and over again. However, just after Christmas, something did alter. One night, when we were in my room, he pulled something out of his pocket.

'Look,' he said to me. 'Look what I've got.'

He showed me a packet – but I had no idea what it was. He took a smaller package out of the box and rolled his eyes when I still looked confused about what he was showing me.

'They're rubbers!' he said excitedly. I had never seen a condom before. I was thirteen years old and I'd been forced into sex since I was four, but I'd had no sex education.

'What are they?' I asked, desperate for anything to distract him. I didn't know what he was showing me but, whatever it was, I'd talk about it all night rather than suffer the usual horrors.

'Do you know nothing?' he scoffed.

I shook my head.

'They're to stop you having a bairn,' he told me.

'What do you mean?' I asked. 'What do they do?'

He was the one looking confused now.

'Well, I put them on and then you don't get a bairn,' he said. I got the feeling that was the sum total of his knowledge on the subject.

'Put them on? What do you mean?' I asked again.

'I put one of *these* on *there* . . .' he whispered, unzipping his trousers and taking out his erection. 'Then . . . well, then you don't get a bairn.'

I was horrified. Condoms back then were made of thick rubber. They smelled disgusting and they weren't made for comfort. I was almost used to the physical act of the abuse by now, as it had happened so often over the years and I was getting older too, but once Jed started using condoms, it hurt again for a while.

He knew how to put them on so I could only think that someone else, maybe one of his brothers, had showed him what to do. Had he told them he had a 'girlfriend'? Did any of them suspect it was me? I had no idea.

Not long after he started using them, the pain and friction I felt from this new approach gave me the courage to try and raise the hideous issue with Granny again. When we were alone in the kitchen I took a deep breath and began.

'Granny,' I said, tentatively. 'I need to talk to you about something. Something bad.'

'What have you done?' she asked, immediately blaming me for whatever was coming.

'Nothing! Nothing! It's not me, it's . . .' I didn't really know how to say this. I didn't know which words to use.

'Is it about my Jed?' she snapped. 'It better not be. I'm warning you, lassie, I'm warning you.'

She had warned me plenty of times in the past too, but I needed to try again.

'Aye,' I said, trying to be brave. 'It's about Jed.'

She narrowed her eyes at me, as if challenging me to say something about her precious boy. 'You mind your step.'

'Jed's been doing bad things,' I whispered. 'To me. Jed's been doing bad things to me.'

She flew across the kitchen like a woman possessed and I felt the full force of the back of her hand slapping me across my jaw at lightning speed.

'You shut up!' she shouted. 'My Jed's got French letters! There's no chance of you having a bairn, so what are you complaining about?'

That was it.

She knew.

If she was linking the contraception to him and then linking it to me, she *knew* what he did to me.

Nothing was the same after that. Just by those words, I realised how little I meant to her. It was as if I was a sacrifice for her son.

It was just day after day of the same thing. Jed trying to get me. Jed raping me. Jed forcing me in the pigeon loft.

My favourite way of escape from all of it was through animals – if I couldn't be with them, I wanted to read about them. No matter what type – dogs, horses, cats, the amazing creatures I read about who lived all over the world – I was drawn to them. I trusted animals and they seemed to trust me. While I hated pigeons, for good reason, I would never harm them, and the very thought of anyone being cruel to an animal horrified me. Perhaps I saw their vulnerability and made a link with my own situation, perhaps I liked that I could tell them anything and never be judged; whatever the reason, animals became my passion and my refuge.

We were still living in the same house on the farm, although we had knocked another cottage into ours for more living space. At the end of the row lived a woman in her fifties called Hetty Black.

I really liked Hetty. She was safe, and that was what mattered more to me than anything else in the world. I went there for a chat whenever I could. Her house was warm and it was comforting. She always treated me the way I needed to be treated, as if she could sense what would be best for me. Some days she would seem to know that I needed to be a child, and she'd feed me, give me nice things to eat, and sit me down by the fire, while she pottered around. On other occasions she spoke to me as if I was a woman, telling me about her life and her relationship as if we were equals. She was always so nice to me.

Hetty had a boyfriend, a man called Tam Lownie, who came and went on some timetable they had agreed between them. They weren't married, they didn't 'live in sin', but everyone knew that they belonged to each other. Tam was one of the first men I ever trusted and he was a good man. He achieved that status in my eyes largely through having a horse and being very kind to it. Tam was never a bad man to me.

One day, when I was sitting with Hetty, he came in unannounced.

'Hello, Sheena!' he cried. 'I'm glad you're here. I've got something for you.'

I looked quickly at Hetty, and reassured myself that she was still sitting there, with no intention of moving, before I risked smiling at Tam. It was so hard to trust anyone – especially men who said that they had things for me.

He always wore a long, multi-pocketed coat, thick with dirt and concealing all sorts of things – from one of those pockets he produced a book. It was called *A Tale of Two Horses*. He passed it over to me and I shyly flicked through the pages.

'Do you like it?' he asked.

I could only nod.

'You're daft on the horses, aren't you?' he laughed. 'It's a long time since I read a book and it'll be longer still before I do so again but when I saw that I thought I knew just the wee lassie who would like it.'

'Thanks, Tam,' I whispered, holding the book close to my chest. 'Thanks so much.'

'Ach . . . you're welcome. Now, Hetty – is that kettle going to put itself on?' he asked, a little embarrassed by how his gift had been received.

They both went to the kitchen and left me there, at the fire, safe and warm, with a book about horses. I couldn't think of anything better.

It was the start of Tam bringing me all sorts of things – all of them with a horse theme. He had some contact who got him 'antiques' as he called them (junk, really) and he would often come into Hetty's house with something in one of his pockets for me. I adored a brooch he gave me at one point, which was in the shape of a riding crop, and I wish I still had it, as it would remind me of two of the kindest people I ever met.

One day, as we sat at her fireside, Hetty said to me, 'Sheena, do you know about men and women?'

'Oh aye,' I told her. 'Auntie Maisie told me.' Maisie was the wife of one of my uncles and she had given me a speech just before I started high school about the birds and the bees. I think she probably assumed that no one would get round to telling me and that, since I didn't have my mum nearby, she should step into the breach. I think she was preparing me for what I might hear at 'big' school, but she wasn't far from useless.

'Sheena,' she'd stammered. 'You need to know something.'

I looked at her with big eyes and she refused to make eye contact.

'You've seen the cows and the bull, haven't you?' she asked.

I nodded. Of course I had. I'd lived on a farm all of my life.

'Well, that's what happens with men and women. Do you understand?'

I nodded again, but she made no sense. She was so embarrassed that I didn't dare ask her to elaborate.

'So – you know that now. And . . . well . . . there's something else. There's something called "periods" . . .'

'That's fine, Auntie Maisie,' I interrupted, trying to save her blushes. 'I know about those. I've got them.'

'Oh. Fine. Fine. Well, there you go. That's you sorted,' she said, rushing away as quickly as she could, sure that she had imparted all of her biological wisdom to me.

No one had actually warned me about periods in advance. I knew nothing when it all started one day at school and it was left to another girl to put me straight. When I went home and told Granny Morag she went ballistic.

'Christ, that's all I need!' she shouted. 'You're a dirty wee bitch, do you know that? Right – you better watch yourself, that's all I can say. Watch yourself and don't get into any trouble. Christ . . .' She walked away muttering and leaving me none the wiser.

She was hardly sympathetic and didn't even ask me what had happened. In actual fact it had all been horrible. I had always bl d quite a lot from 'down there' because of the abuse. When I w t to the toilet one day in school and saw the quantity of blood on my knickers, I thought I was dying from what Jed had done to me.

I thought he had given me cancer.

Of course, that made no sense, but you have to remember that I knew nothing. Sexual abuse had been part of my life within my own family since I was little more than a baby. I was always sore and always bleeding. That day it was even worse and I truly believed that I had been infected with something awful because of it.

I started crying in the cubicle. A feisty girl I knew called Jane Trotter came in and asked what was wrong. I sniffed and told her that I was dying and needed to get to a doctor. She told me to let her in, which I did, and she closed the door behind her. Peering at my knickers, she scoffed, 'You're not dying, that's just normal.'

'What?' I asked. 'Normal? How can it be normal?'

'It's what's supposed to happen. It's your period. I've had mine since I was ten,' she said.

'But what is it?' I asked, completely ignorant of my own biology despite the ravages inflicted on my body by others.

'It comes every month,' Jane said. 'It's because you're not getting a baby. It's fine. Come on – you'll live.'

She shoved a big wad of toilet paper in my knickers and took me to the school nurse. Jane was right. I lived. However, it was an eye-opener for me. Until that point, I knew nothing but I started asking a few questions, nothing so obvious that it would draw attention to me, but enough (combined with reading and watching) to work out what was going on. Before then I hadn't linked what Eddie or Jed were doing with the making of babies. I hadn't sussed out that the act they forced on me created children. When you grow up on a farm you know the basics as you see the animals, but it didn't equate to humans for me. Those animals were in a field and it was done with no nonsense, but it was different for people, surely? From that point I started to be much more aware, although I was still very much alone.

On that day with Hetty things changed. For the first time I felt as if someone really noticed me. When she asked if I knew about men and women and I said that Maisie had told me, she didn't stop there.

'What about other things?' she asked.

'What other things?' I replied.

She sighed and took my hand. 'Sheena – I have to ask you this, hen. Has anybody been touching you?'

I panicked.

I couldn't believe she was asking me such a thing. How could she know? How could she know what was happening?

I shook my head frantically but she pulled me close to her.

'Sheena, Sheena, listen to me. We need to get the polis, hen.'

'No! No!' I shouted, terrified. 'They'll take the house off us, Hetty, they'll take the house off us.'

'What do you mean?' she asked. 'What has the house got to do with it?'

I was simply repeating what had been drummed into me ever since I could remember. Granny Morag had always said that Jed was simple, and that if I told anyone what he was doing I'd get the jail and we'd lose the house. Everyone would be homeless and we'd have nothing if I didn't protect Jed.

I had to tell Hetty my fears. As the tears flowed and I told her what would happen, she shook her head and the anger flared in her eyes.

'You can't get the jail, you can't get the jail,' she said over and over, rocking me in her arms. 'You've done nothing wrong.'

'It's not his fault,' I said. 'He can't help doing the bad things.'

'Who?' she demanded. 'Who's doing the bad things?'

I couldn't say his name, I couldn't break the family up by telling the truth.

'Eddie Johnstone,' I said quietly.

'Eddie Johnstone?' she repeated. 'How could he make you lose the house? What does your granny's house have to do with him? Do you even see him now? Betty's moved – and she's divorced, isn't she?'

It was true. Auntie Betty had divorced by now and there were no family links with the Johnstones.

'I see you going into the pigeon loft,' said Hetty quietly. 'I hear you crying, hen.'

She knew. She knew it was Jed but she wanted me to say it. I guess she must have thought that if I admitted it she could take action on my behalf.

'It's our Jed,' I wept. 'Jed does the bad things.'

'How often?' she asked.

'Every day. No matter where I go or what I do he's there. He always wants to do it, he always wants to do the bad things.'

'And Morag knows about this?' she asked through gritted teeth.

'It's not her fault,' I said. 'It's not his fault. He's simple, Hetty.'

'Oh aye, he's that simple that he's kept a job down for years. He's that simple that he always has money and is the apple of his mother's eye. He's that simple that he's the one with the job that keeps a roof over all your heads.' As I said before, the house was tied to Jed's work on the farm. 'He's that bloody simple that he does whatever he does to you every day and yet you're the one that has to keep quiet about it – if he was so bloody stupid he'd be telling everyone, wouldn't he? He wouldn't be able to keep his mouth shut if he was really poor simple Jed,' she finished.

'Hetty,' I ventured. 'Please don't tell anyone.'

'You won't go to jail,' she said again. 'You've done nothing wrong. We'll get the polis and we'll get this sorted out once and for all.'

'No! No, please don't! I made it all up, Hetty! It isn't true!' I shrieked, desperate for her to keep my secret. As much as I wanted the abuse to stop, I didn't believe that I wasn't to blame and I truly did think that we would all suffer if I told the police. The threat of jail for me loomed large no matter Hetty's words. It had been ingrained into me for so long that I couldn't simply shake it off, no matter how kind my neighbour was.

'That's fine,' she said, ignoring my pathetic attempts to backtrack. 'We'll still go to the police because they'll be able to find out what the truth is.'

I begged and begged her to believe me, to believe that I was lying, and when that didn't work I told the truth. I admitted what Jed was doing but pleaded with her to tell no one.

'They'll get you, Hetty,' I said. 'You're on your own and Tam's not here all the time – they'll do something to you. No one will talk to you if you get involved, and you know they're capable of things – things that I don't want to see happen to you. Please, Hetty. You're my friend and I don't want to lose you. Please keep this to yourself.'

She did.

I don't know what it cost her to keep quiet but she managed. She barely ever spoke to my family again, but she was always there for me with a cup of tea and a smile if I sought her out. Every time I went into the pigeon loft I wondered if she was watching. It was never the same between us. Looking back, I don't know what to think. Should she have ignored me and gone to the police? As a grown woman I'd say, yes, of course she should have, but those were different times and there's no guarantee the police would have believed either of us. Her life would have been a misery, she would have been ostracised and I do honestly believe that one of Morag's sons would have gone after her. Who's to say what was the right thing to do?

All I knew was that nothing had really changed – Jed was still doing what he wanted to me, whenever he wanted, and all I could do was accept it.

Chapter 17

None so blind

The social workers still came out to the house on a regular basis but I was never allowed to speak to them on my own. Granny Morag made sure of that.

They were brought into the cottage, given a cup of tea and a biscuit, and 'shown' me as if I were an exhibit that had to be presented very briefly then ignored. As always, as she had done ever since I was a very little girl, she was quick to tell them what a liar I was. She said the same things every time. You would think that the social workers would have got wise to her, but perhaps they just assumed that because what she said never deviated it must be the truth.

I wanted to plead with them to take me away, but I never got a chance. They would sit there, cup of tea in hand, while Granny told them what a liar I was, what a bad girl I was, what a terrible burden I was. Then she'd sigh and become the martyr, saying dramatically how she could never throw me out, how I was her own flesh and blood, how – no matter how hard I made it – she'd do her best. Impressed, they would drink their tea, eat their biscuit, make their notes, and leave me to my fate yet again.

It was getting worse. It wasn't that the abuse was worse, it was the fact that I was getting older, more aware of things, and hurtling towards adulthood. When I was very little I didn't know what was going on. That excuses nothing, but as I grew up I knew this wasn't right, I knew it wasn't happening to every child and more than ever I wanted it to stop.

One day, when I was peeling potatoes for our evening meal, I cut my finger. It wasn't a terribly bad cut, but the blood held my attention as it seeped onto one of the tatties lying on the chopping board. As the bright red spread across the peeled potato, I was mesmerised. Images of Jed flashed into my mind and I picked up the knife. Holding it in my hand, I turned it round thinking of him, thinking of the damage it could do to him.

I heard Granny Morag coming through to the kitchen, so I quickly scraped the peelings into a bowl ready to be thrown into the waste for the pigs. I filled the saucepan with cold water and put it, with the tatties, on the hob. Just as she came into the room I opened the door.

'Just taking the peelings out!' I called.

The knife was in the pocket of my cardigan. I could feel it lying heavily as I walked, and I knew that I wouldn't be putting it back.

That night I lay in bed, staring at it. The moon shone in through my bedroom window and the blade glistened as dreams of Jed hurtled through my mind. I wanted to stab him. I wanted to hurt him. I did. I wanted it so badly.

The next night I heard Granny Morag rummaging around in the kitchen drawer.

'Where's the knife?' she asked.

'What knife?' I casually replied.

She tutted. 'The wee sharp red one. The one for tatties.'

'No idea,' I said.

'Well, you must have used it last,' she retorted. 'You peeled the tatties last night, you must have used it then.'

The lie was out of my mouth before I had even thought of it. 'No,' I said. 'No. I couldn't find it either. I used the black one. Maybe Jed's been using it for something.'

She cursed and went on with her business as I fingered the handle of the 'missing' knife in my pocket. Just having it there comforted me but I was never strong enough to use it. Each day I told myself that I would. Each time he sent me to the pigeon loft to wait for him, I tried to pluck up the courage to take the knife with me, but I never had that badness which seemed to run through so much of my family. So I never did stab Jed.

One day, I returned to my room after he had done his usual things to me. The knife was hidden under a pile of clothes in a drawer, and I pulled it out, desperate for the small shred of comfort it gave me. I sat there weeping quietly and hurting as always. I was completely unaware of Granny Morag standing behind me.

'You lying little bitch!' she screeched, grabbing the knife from me. 'You said you had no idea where it was! You tried to blame it on my poor Jed! You evil little bitch!'

She was soon distracted from the knife itself by the energy she had to put in to hammering me. Granny was getting older but her appetite for violence where I was concerned showed no sign of diminishing. Afterwards she was always out of breath and red in the face, but she seemed to get so much pleasure from beating me that I don't think she would ever have stopped voluntarily.

I was bigger than her by that point, and I could have defended myself better, but I knew it would only have made things worse. We all had our roles to play in that house and my role was whipping girl for Granny and plaything for Jed. I was getting fat by that point and when I was thirteen Granny Morag took me to the doctor.

'You're a state,' she said. 'Size of a fucking house.'

The doctor put me on a drug called Ponderax, a now-notorious slimming pill which was prescribed from the mid-1960s and is now believed to have caused heart-valve problems in many people. It was basically an amphetamine and banned some years ago because of the potential dangers of long-term use. There was little need for me to take it at that stage of my life. I had puppy fat but the main problem was the constant diet of sweets as 'shut up' bribes from Jed. I ate them constantly and soon fell into a pattern of bad eating habits. Food became my escape from my own life. I would eat anything and everything, stealing it from the kitchen when no one was looking and spending the money Jed gave me when he abused me on more food. It was a vicious cycle and it also added to the bullying I was suffering at school.

There was one ray of light at school, one teacher who made a difference. Her name was Dr MacDonald, and she knew so much about so many things. She was my hero. Dr MacDonald was a fusty old woman who belted kids without a flicker, but she also had a soft spot for me. She knew that I loved the classics, just like her, and she did what she could to encourage that love. I wanted to be like her and I started to read everything I could get my hands on, hoping, just hoping that it might give me a way out. Reading became my obsession, just as Jed had his.

I was clever but my work suffered. I didn't want to go to school as I was called so many names, and I also had a well-deserved reputation for not doing homework, which got me into trouble almost every day. The reason behind that was simple. Every time I escaped to a room to work, I would be followed by Jed who would start up his usual attacks on me.

When I was about fourteen, things came to a head. I'm not too sure how it was all decided – I think that Dr MacDonald, my adored teacher, may have been involved – but Granny Morag was called in to school and told that I was causing them concern. By this stage I was still putting on a lot of weight, through a com-bination of comfort eating and being bribed by Jed, and I had stopped taking the slimming pills as they had horrible side effects, such as hallucinations. I didn't need any more horror in my life, so I flushed the tablets down the toilet and the weight piled on. On top of the obvious physical problems I was having I was a bit of a loose cannon with no real friends. I was disconnected from everything and someone must have finally noticed the signs.

I came back from school one day and Granny Morag was sit-ting at the kitchen table with a face like thunder. She had been to school for a meeting with the head teacher and was clearly furi-ous about something.

'You've to go see someone,' she announced.

'What do you mean?' I asked.

'I don't know what's wrong with you, Sheena. I've given up my life for you, you've got everything a lassie could ever wish for, and yet you're acting like a bloody lunatic. You're drawing attention to yourself and shaming this family.' She shook her head in annoyance at me.

'So what's going to happen?' I questioned her.

'You've to see a doctor,' she replied.

'For more slimming pills?' I asked warily.

'Oh no – no, that's too bloody normal for you, isn't it?' she snapped. 'You ... YOU ... have to go see someone at the loony bin.'

'The loony bin?' I repeated.

'Aye, the fucking loony bin. You shame this family, you do, you shame us all.'

'Do you mean the Andrew Duncan?'

'I certainly do. Are you happy now?' With that, she stormed out of the room.

I knew my life was awful, I knew that I wanted Jed to stop, and I had known for some time that what he did to me was very, very wrong – but the Andrew Duncan? The very name had so many connotations. At that time (and, actually, to this day) the Royal Edinburgh Hospital was where anyone with a severe mental health problem was sent. The specific ward was called the Andrew Duncan Clinic and to be sent there came with huge stigma. In fact, anything to do with mental health issues was stigmatised. 'Normal' people didn't go there, 'normal' people just got on with things. If someone in your family did have a breakdown or was suffering from depression or any other mental health challenge, it was ignored, swept under the carpet, and never spoken about. My behaviour had brought things out into the open and for that I was seen as bringing shame on the family. The irony was, of course, that after what had been done to me I should have been screaming from the rooftops, drawing attention to just what awful things had been perpetrated by those two men. Instead, almost without knowing it, my behaviour had drawn attention all by itself. I was too fat, too odd, too disconnected. Because of all those things I was finally facing the prospect that someone would listen to me.

The appointment to meet with a psychiatrist came a few weeks later. While waiting on it Granny had barely been civil to me. All of her comments had been her usual ones about me bringing shame on her and the family, and about how she would never live this down. Of course, it was only the fact that she was telling everyone that I was to be referred to the 'loony bin' that made them aware of it in the first place!

One night, I was woken by the noise of arguing coming from the front room. Betty had been round to see her mum, and I had gone to bed quite early as it was clear that they didn't want me there. It was about ten o'clock and I could hear a low mumble as they spoke. I got up and tiptoed through, listening at the door. I couldn't catch everything they said but they were clearly talking about me and my upcoming appointment. What I did hear were things such as:

She better not say anything.
You'll have to have a word before she goes.
Tell them she's a liar – tell them she makes things up.

We were back to that. Back to me being labelled as the liar of the family while Betty and Granny did all they could to get their version of things in first. I crept back to bed and thought about it. When I went to the appointment what would I say? Would I tell the doctor everything? Would I finally pluck up the courage to reveal what had been happening to me for years?

I thought I would. I thought I would take this chance.

I lay there that night, and all the nights that followed, and ran it through my mind. I made my decision. The decision to tell.

The morning of the appointment dawned bright and sunny. Granny Morag made me some breakfast and put her coat on as I ate.

'Are you taking me to the bus?' I asked.

She stared at me as if I was completely clueless.

'I'm going with you,' she said.

I gulped. I didn't want her there. I didn't know if I could go through with it if she was waiting outside for me.

'I can manage,' I said weakly.

'No. No, you can't. You need to take two buses and you'll never find it on your own. Plus, I don't want you walking around with all those nutters loose. It's not safe for a young lassie.'

This was just the sort of thing I expected Granny to say. The nutters, the dangerous men who were unsafe around a young lassie, lived in my house. She should have been protecting me there rather than telling me that Jed was a poor soul who was just lonely.

'Really, I'll be fine,' I persisted.

'Not on your nelly,' she said. 'Hurry up. We don't want to be late for your *special* doctor now, do we?'

I trailed behind her as we went to the appointment but I still hoped I would be brave enough when we got there, brave enough to tell the doctor what was going on.

The building wasn't as intimidating as I had thought it would be. It was set in a posh residential area in lovely gardens. The receptionist was very friendly and told us that Dr Smith would be with us shortly. As Granny Morag and I sat waiting I looked around for evidence of the 'nutters' she had warned me of. There were none to be seen. A few old men shuffled about, but they didn't look mad. There were some other people waiting, but they seemed normal. They were dressed in what appeared to be their Sunday clothes and everyone was very wary of making eye contact with each other.

Granny Morag sat with her handbag on her lap and a scowl on her face. She was still ashamed, as she had told me on the journey there, but she also seemed to be reasonably calm.

The receptionist called to me – 'Dr Smith will see you now' – and I stood up to follow her pointing finger down a corridor lined with paintings.

Granny Morag got up too.

'I don't think I'll be long,' I told her, walking away.

She followed me.

'What are you doing?' I asked. 'Where are you going?'

'I'm coming with you, of course,' she replied.

No! No, she couldn't do this!

'I'll be fine,' I told her, trying to keep my voice steady.

'I couldn't care less how you'll be,' she said. 'I'm coming with you.'

When we walked into the room, Dr Smith said nothing. He simply motioned towards two chairs and we sat down. He continued writing something in his folder, then turned to us, sighing as he removed his glasses and rubbed his temples.

'Miss Harrison—' he began.

'I'm her granny,' came a solid, commanding voice from beside me.

'Yes, quite—'

'I'm her granny and I'll be talking first,' she stated.

'Will you now,' he replied, bemused.

'Aye, I will – there's things you need to know about our Sheena,' she began. 'She's no' right, she's no' . . . all there.'

'Is that so?' the doctor asked.

'Aye. So, you see, you're wasting your time. She's a fantasist. She lies. She makes things up. So, it's probably best that you just give her something and we'll be on our way.'

The doctor looked at her. I said nothing as I listened to my granny's oft-repeated lines and reflected on what I'd overheard between her and Betty.

'Is there anything you'd like to tell me, Sheena?' he asked. I noticed that he only remembered my name by checking his notes again.

I shook my head.

He sighed deeply. 'Well, there must be *some* reason why you're here. So what is it?'

'There's nothing. *I've* told you,' said Granny Morag.

The psychiatrist just stared at me. I swallowed hard and closed my eyes.

'There is something,' I said quietly. 'I am upset about something.'

'Lies!' shouted Granny. 'Lies!'

Dr Smith stared at her. She pursed her lips and said nothing. He looked very cross, but I needed to continue despite neither of them seeming to want to hear me.

'It's something at home . . .'

I heard Granny take a deep breath and saw the doctor fire her a look again.

'Go on,' he said.

'Well, I live with my Uncle Jed and he . . . and he . . .'

I didn't really know what to say or what words to use.

A sigh of exasperation came from the psychiatrist as he snapped, 'He what?'

'I'm sorry, Granny, but I have to say . . . Uncle Jed—'

Before I could finish the back of her hand slapped me across the face with such force that I was pushed backwards in my seat.

'Don't you start running my Jed down! Don't you start telling lies about him!' she screamed. 'And you!' she said, turning to the doctor as she dragged me out of the chair. 'You shouldn't listen to evil lassies like her. Getting them in here and asking them, *asking them*, to tell you lies! It's a disgrace, that's what it is, a disgrace!'

She slapped me again for good measure then bent down to pick her handbag off the floor.

I looked towards Dr Smith, who seemed to be in shock. I sent out a silent prayer that he would put Granny in her place and ask me to tell my story, in private, with him alone.

'Really ... this is quite ... I have no idea ...' he stuttered. 'Actually, I think ... yes, I must ask you to leave. This is quite unacceptable. Please leave. Please leave at once.'

'Oh, we'll leave, all right!' shouted the old woman, heading for the door. 'And you can rest assured that we won't be back. She's a wicked lassie, wicked!'

With that, she bundled me out – out of the room, out of the hospital, and back towards home.

'You were warned.' That was all she said to me, until we arrived back at the cottage. 'You were warned.'

As I rushed to my room, the tears flowing down my cheeks, I could only think of another of her favourite sayings – *there's none so blind as those who will not see.*

Chapter 18

Sanctuary

Granny Morag was still in her own bedroom. It was her sanctuary but the rest of us were allowed in, even if we had to maintain the pretence that no one ever crossed the threshold. There was one main reason for going in there – she had a huge stash of treats. There were drawers full of biscuits (good ones in individual wrappers, not just big packs of broken ones) and heaps of chocolate. There were glass bottles of 'juice' (or 'pop') lined up along the window ledges. It was delivered weekly by a van which went round all of the houses and it came in all sorts of flavours. Every so often I would go in and have some of the raspberry or cola from an opened bottle, but everyone knew that they could never touch the limeade as that was for Granny alone. She knew what we were up to – given that they were all empty at the end of the week when the van came round again – but it was one thing she turned a blind eye to.

Sneaking into her room to pinch a bar of chocolate or a quick sip of raspberry drink was one of the few pleasures I had. If I knew she had gone out for a while, it was even better because I could take my time choosing which of the treats I would select and then savour it. I remember one Saturday morning when she left with the pillowcases slung over her shoulders – a sure sign that it would be ages before she got back. About an hour after she left, I tiptoed into her room and got a big bar of Fry's chocolate. I made it last for ages and savoured every drop. It tasted even better because I'd managed to keep away from Jed that morning and I was pretending that I had a perfect, uneventful life.

Granny still wasn't back at lunchtime and, even after some toast, my tummy was rumbling. The snow was whirling outside the windows and I decided to risk another venture into her room, convincing myself that she would be even longer than usual in this weather. I had my eye on some chocolate peanuts she had and thought that I could just take a handful and run back to my own room in case she did turn up.

I thought there was no one else in the house as they were all working in the fields and byres after lunch, but no sooner had I opened a drawer than I heard footsteps behind me.

Jed.

'Are you eating again?' he said. I was eating as much as I could and it was all heavy, stodgy food. On top of that all my uncles and aunties gave me sweets, as did Jed when he wanted to bribe me if he thought I might say something to someone about what he was doing. I was also going into Granny's room for more and more stolen treats whenever I could. Of course, I now know that I was setting myself up for a lifetime of eating problems. To this day I have issues with food, and it all stems from those early years when I was bribed with sweets and also comforted myself by eating as much as possible.

'I'm just getting a wee something,' I told him.

'You'll burst one day,' he replied. 'Anyway, if you want sweeties I'll give you some.'

I shook my head. I wanted nothing from him. I'd rather pinch what Granny had hidden.

'My sweeties not good enough for you?' he sneered.

I pushed the drawer closed and got up from where I had been kneeling with my haul. I headed towards the door, but as I passed Jed he pushed me onto Granny Morag's big bed.

'Not so fast . . .' he said.

'No, Jed – she'll be back soon. Let me go!' I cried.

'She'll be ages,' he replied. 'And anyway – even if she's not . . . so what?'

'You'll get into trouble!' I tried to warn him, hoping it would be enough for him to waver and let me go.

'No, *you'll* get into trouble,' he snorted.

He got onto the bed beside me and pulled my knickers off. I squirmed around and, uncharacteristically, screamed. I never usually made any noise because there was no point. Although I knew there was no one to hear me now I still felt this was even worse than usual. The very thought that he would consider raping me in Granny's bed seemed a step too far even for Jed.

I was making such a racket, telling him to stop over and over – and then, suddenly, I was aware of the bedroom door opening.

I turned to look.

Standing there was Granny Morag.

She must have heard me screaming.

There was no way she could misinterpret what was happening – I was on the bed, upset and bellowing with my knickers on the floor beside me and Jed on top with his trousers at his ankles, touching me, ready to abuse me.

I met her eyes and looked pleadingly at this woman who had told me I was so damned lucky that she had taken me in. So lucky that she had given me a home. So lucky to be loved by all of them.

She didn't say a word.

She closed the door and walked away.

My own granny walked away from her fifteen-year-old granddaughter being raped by her own son. Something shattered in me that day – hope, I think.

The next day she gave me some crisps and a bottle of juice from her own stash.

'You're a good lassie,' she said. 'You stay in here with me while I read my *People's Friend*.'

I did. I was so grateful for any crumb of kindness that I took what I could get, even if it was a packet of crisps and some pop for the fact that she had seen me being abused by her own son in her bed. It wasn't so different from Eddie taking me to the play park and giving me a biscuit all those years ago.

There was a box with legs at the side of her bed and, after a while, she took out all of the old photos from it, and started going through them, showing me my mother and talking to me warmly.

I could never remember her being like that before.

'Now, you be good to Jed,' she went on. 'We could lose the

house if he gets put away, because who would bring the money in? You remember that – he's the one who keeps this family together.'

No, I thought.

I am.

I'm the one who keeps all of your dirty little secrets. I'm the one who pays for the perversions. I'm the one who takes all of the abuse, sexual, physical and emotional. I'm the one who keeps this family together when maybe it would be better falling apart.

I thought I could hear someone out in the hall that day while I sat with my own grandmother and she justified why I should keep quiet about her son raping me. I think he was listening. I think they both did what they wanted with me and I was nothing to them, not in the grand scale of things.

I was terrified now that I was having my periods. Jed said that it would be fine and even that the rubbers were a great idea because we could have sex when I was menstruating and he wouldn't get any blood on him. He must have had access to hundreds given how often he raped me. The laddies all had them, and I think granny bought them so that she didn't get any pregnant girlfriends turning up on her doorstep.

The condoms back then were brown and smelled like vile dirty rubber, not thin like nowadays. There was a white-coloured sort of bulb on the end and Jed used to make me put them on him after a while. He showed me what to do; I had to hold the bulb so that it didn't get air in it, then roll it on. If I hurt him he'd say, 'Watch what you're doing, you stupid bitch!' I was a bag of nerves at the thought of getting pregnant from him and God knows how I didn't at first; he was there so often. Perversely, I think that somebody must have been looking out for me. If there is a God maybe he was thinking *That poor child*.

Sometimes, Jed would jump off after he had ejaculated and the sperm would fall out of the rubber, going all over my legs or bed. That caused trouble as there were obvious stains. Granny would shout at me, saying, 'You've pished on the bed, you dirty wee bitch!' and I would just take it, both of us knowing full well what had caused the mark.

Every time I got my period I was relieved.

I always knew it was coming because I would get a little sick the day before and get pain, but I welcomed that as it meant I was safe for that month. It was like someone had lifted a ton weight from me.

When Jed couldn't get a rubber, he got a plastic bag that had held fruit or something, and he'd cover himself with that instead. Once he used a bread wrapper. He would cut the insides of a cornflake packet if he had to. He knew what he was doing, that took thought. When he used things like that it was really sore and it scratched. After those occasions I was bleeding.

It all blended into one after a while. There were times when I was so desperate to get it over and done with that I would ask Jed if he wanted me to help him read his pigeon books. How awful is that? How bad were things when I was the one trying to get the abuse over and done with so that I could be left alone?

And then, one day, it just stopped.

I don't know what day it was because I didn't know it had stopped until it had been the case for a while, if that makes sense.

But it did. It stopped. I think, in retrospect, he just lost interest because I was growing up. I was a young woman. I wasn't a child any more and I couldn't feed that part of what he wanted. Things went by in a daze for a while because I couldn't quite believe it was over. There was also part of me that remembered how relieved I had been after Eddie had gone from my life and yet Jed came along soon after; maybe someone else would fill the gap now.

They didn't.

Not in that way.

But I did meet someone – Ewan. Someone who finally made me realise that there was more to love and sex than I had ever experienced so far.

There were a few boys before Ewan though – I had absolutely no respect for myself given what I had been through and I certainly had a 'reputation' in the village. Sex was my only currency, and I had started sleeping with other boys when I was fourteen. They took advantage of the fact that there was a girl who would have sex with them if they asked her to, and I hated it from the start but I didn't know how else to act. I had never known any different.

I wasn't popular exactly, but I did have something which bought me friends – money. Everyone else in the family was working and they all gave me cash. At the weekend I would easily have twenty pounds in my purse from various family members and that was a fortune back then when a tenner was a week's wages. I remember events like the local gala day when there would be a crowd of lads and lassies. I'd be tagging along, with them but not with them. On the fringes until someone needed something, then suddenly I'd be their best pal. I always had plenty of friends when I had money – though when the money went so did they. I treated them all to whatever they wanted and I was known for it.

It soon went further than sweets and chips and rides at the fair – it moved on to sex. I'd always end up with the one no one else wanted. I don't even remember the first boy. I do know that it was round the back of the caravans and that it didn't feel any different, it was just more of the same.

Until Ewan.

I liked him, that was the only difference – there was no difference in the act itself, no pleasure for me, but I didn't feel as bad afterwards as with him I had made a choice. I didn't just go with him for the sake of it. He had never tried to touch me, he had always treated me like I was a friend, one of the boys, and I appreciated that so much.

We would spend whole days together, with a bag full of sandwiches in the summer, lying by the side of the river, just talking. Eventually I started to open up to him and I told him what I'd been through. He never asked for details, he just supported me. He was gorgeous and I couldn't believe that he was there for me; he used to listen so well, and I had never had that before.

'You'll be old enough to get away soon,' Ewan said to me one day. 'That's what you need to do – get away from them all.'

He was right. He was so, so right.

Chapter 19

The ride to freedom

I used to get the *Horse & Hound* magazine just to look at the pictures of the beautiful beasts. I'd never be able to afford one but I liked to dream. One day, as I was reading the For Sale pages, it ran into a new section. They must have had extra ads that week – and it must have been fate. As I kept reading, I was in the Situations Vacant page before I knew it.

A big advert stood out.

Grooms were wanted in Cornwall.

Immediately I thought *I could do that.*

There was a number to call and I ran across the road straight away, pretending to Granny that I was off to listen to Dial-a-Disc.

I spoke to the woman in charge and told her what I knew about horses. I wasn't as good a rider as I could have been as I hurt every time I rode due to the damage that had been done by the abuse, but I was still pretty good. The woman said that she would take me through my trek leader's certificate if I wanted the job – I could work with horses all the time! It was like a dream come true. There was no interview, they just took me at my word – but I still had to get past Granny Morag and that seemed insurmountable.

I knew I'd have to give up my dream of studying English but it would be worth it. When the woman at the stables – Patricia – asked if I could make my way there on Monday, I almost fainted.

'This Monday?' I asked.

'Yes – this Monday,' she replied.

'The next Monday that happens?' I asked daftly.

She laughed. 'Yes, that's the one!'

I had a week.

A week to escape – but a week in which my dreams could also be shattered.

On the Wednesday I told Granny Morag and also said it was too late for her to change my mind. I was picking up my train ticket in Edinburgh on the Monday – it had all been arranged by Patricia. She was livid.

'You can't really expect that this'll happen, can you?' she screamed. 'You're going nowhere. Nowhere at all.'

She was wrong and I told her – but I was all front. She said she'd stop me and I believed her. As we both stood our ground I could see that she wasn't the woman she had once been. My granny was ill and getting weaker. She had been diagnosed with breast cancer after refusing to go to a doctor for years. Every time I saw her she looked smaller; she was physically deteriorating with every passing week. The pain in her arm, which she had complained of for some time, was breast and lung cancer. She had been told to exercise her left arm as the doctor thought it was muscle deterioration but it was actually the cancer spreading upwards. Granny Morag was still smoking incessantly, and she would do so right up until the end. At that time I didn't feel bad about leaving, despite her being obviously unwell; I just wanted away.

The men were all out but I knew she would fall on them as soon as they came back. She no doubt thought she would have a whole cavalry of allies who would all agree with her that I should stay at home – for ever.

'Listen to this! Listen to this!' she shrieked as they walked in. 'This ungrateful wee bitch thinks she's just going to up and leave me. She wants to leave all of us – work with fucking horses, no less; in Cornwall, no less!'

'Well, it's high time the lassie did something,' said Robbie, sighing. 'If she can get a job with horses, fair play to her. It's what she likes, and if she's got someone to train her, that's good.'

'Are you fucking joking?' screamed Granny. 'How is she going to survive on her own? They'll kick her out on her first day, as soon as she starts all her lying and fantasising.'

'No. They won't,' said Freddie calmly. 'She needs to get away, Mother, she's not a bairn any more. Let her go.'

Granny Morag stared at him. 'I can't believe this! Why are you all turning against me? How can I afford to let her go?'

Maybe she wasn't referring to money. If I left, the social work payments would end, and I could only assume that my mum would stop sending money for me too, but perhaps she was talking about something else. If I went, what would happen to Jed? If he really couldn't control himself, if he was so 'simple' that he didn't know what he was doing when he abused me, then there was a chance she thought it might spill over, out of the family. Was it possible that she felt Jed might start attacking girls or women elsewhere? Everyone had to do everything to make his life easy – me more than anyone – and there was a little voice in the back of my head saying that she wasn't trying to keep me from leaving through any feelings for me; she was just trying to keep her precious boy safe as she'd always done.

I hadn't expected the others to be so supportive of me, but the fact that they were made my resolve even stronger. 'I'm going, Granny,' I said, 'I'm going, and you can't stop me.'

'Is that a fact?' she snapped. 'You're just going to head off, are you? Not a penny to your name and nowhere to go?'

'But I do have somewhere to go – the stables are sending me a train ticket. It'll be waiting for me at Waverley Station on Monday, and I do have money.' I always had money. Jed was always giving me money, paying me off, and all of my other uncles slipped me cash here and there. She was running out of reasons and excuses.

'We'll give you money anyway,' said Robbie. 'Take her into Edinburgh tomorrow, Mum, and get her everything she needs. This is her chance – don't spoil it for her.' I could have wept with gratitude for their kindness. Jed was standing beside Robbie and Freddie, saying nothing, just staring at the floor and kicking his feet, and Granny Morag looked as if she was deflating in front of us; all of her anger was fading away now that she knew no one was on her side. 'Get her some jodhpurs and nice white shirts, get her a horsey jacket and all the bits she needs. Our Sheena should have everything and we'll pay for it. I want you to go into the shops tomorrow and get her ready, do you understand? Do you understand what I'm saying, Mother?'

It was as if Robbie's words were opening a door for me. I almost let myself believe in that moment that I was going to escape. There was still a small part of me that wondered if it could possibly be true, was I really going to be allowed to leave? Granny's next words gave me even more hope. 'Maybe you're right, son,' she said, very quietly. 'Maybe you're right – maybe it's time to let the lass go.'

She looked towards Jed, and Freddie followed her eyes. 'What do you think, Jed? She should go, shouldn't she, Jed? Sheena should get away and make something of herself, isn't that right?' I don't think Freddie had a clue. He was a lovely man, nothing more than a big, happy, silly boy in a grown-up's body, and I think if he had known what Jed was doing to me he would have stepped in.

Jed was caught between a rock and a hard place. 'If you think so, Freddie, if you think she should go, then maybe she should – but won't she be awfully lonely? What if she gets into trouble?'

'She'll be fine,' answered Freddie. 'Will you chip in as well? Make sure she has everything she needs?'

Jed never took his eyes off the floor. 'If you think that's the best thing, Freddie – I've got twenty pounds. Would you like twenty pounds, Sheena? Would that be awful nice of me to give you that?'

Nice? After what he had done? I thought of all the money he had bribed me with over the years and knew that I would take this last pay-off just as I had taken all of the other ones. The difference would be that, this time, I wouldn't be frittering it away on other people, buying their friendship and then seeing them walk away as soon as the funds ran out; this time I would be using it for my escape. 'That'd be really nice of you, Jed,' I said.

'I'll get it from the drawer,' he said, leaving the room.

'There's fifteen from me,' said Freddie, handing it to his mother.

'You can have whatever I've got on me,' added Robbie, digging into his pockets. I remember to this day how much he handed over – forty-six pounds and a handful of change. It added up to a fortune back then, and my Granny took it all, looking at the money in her hand as if she couldn't quite take in what was going on. I knew she wouldn't give it to me directly and my fear was that she wouldn't keep to her word. If she decided to just hold on to what her sons had donated and act as if the conversation had never happened, would they say anything, or would it all just go back to how it had always been?

The next day, I woke up with a feeling of unease. If Granny stopped all of this from happening – as she so easily could – I didn't know what I would do or how I would go on. I lay there with the sun streaming through the windows of the room which had hosted so many of my living nightmares and listened to the old woman bustling about in the other parts of the house.

After a few minutes I heard her voice. 'Sheena! Sheena! Where are you? Sheena!'

I dragged myself out of bed, already heavy with the disappointment I felt waiting for me, and slowly walked to the kitchen.

Granny Morag was standing there, holding on to the back of a chair with her handbag nestled in the crook of her arm.

'What's keeping you?' she snapped. 'Are you planning to let the folks of Edinburgh have a good laugh at you?'

'What?' I stammered.

'Are we going shopping with you in your nightie and an unwashed face?' she asked. 'Come on – get your arse into gear or we'll miss the bus.'

'We're going?' I whispered. 'We're really going to Edinburgh to get my things?'

She shook her head at me. 'For Christ's sake! After all that nonsense last night? All that money my boys have given you to make sure you've got everything you need? I suppose you've changed your mind?' she said, dramatically sitting down and making as if to unbutton her coat.

'No! No! I just thought . . .' my words tailed off. I didn't want to give her the chance to stop it all from happening, so I flew to my room, calling that I would be back in a few minutes.

I washed quickly and dressed without thinking of what I was wearing. Granny Morag was waiting for me by the door and we walked to the bus stop in the sunshine. I hardly dared speak for fear it would break the spell. She could still find a way to stop me if she wanted to, and she still had that nasty streak in her that could come to the fore at any time.

I don't think I breathed freely until we were in the shop paying for my things. The boots were my pride and joy, brown and shiny with elasticated sides, but I also got two pairs of cream jodhpurs, a handful of white silk polo-neck jumpers, a brown hacking jacket, and a new brown riding hat trimmed with velvet with a bow at the back.

She took me to Jenners for a cream tea and I think that was when we both finally realised it was happening. I was leaving, I was breaking free.

There was no grand farewell on the Monday, no apologies for the years of horror, no scene of forgiveness. I was taken to the station by Robbie and almost screamed with relief when the ticket I had been promised by Patricia was actually waiting there. I don't think anyone had ever promised me anything good before and come through on it.

As the train pulled out of Waverley Station, I said goodbye to everything – to Granny, to Scotland, to the people who had betrayed me, but mostly to my mother. This was it, this was the start of my life. I couldn't rely on her to save me, I never could. This was the beginning of my future. I was finally free.

Chapter 20

Becoming me

Cornwall allowed me to find out who I really was. I had always dreamed of escaping but I had always thought that it would be on a plane to America. The fact that I had managed to get away on my own initiative was miraculous. I played it all over in my mind, thinking of what could have gone wrong – *if I hadn't seen the ad, if I hadn't made the call, if the laddies hadn't supported me, if Granny had put her foot down.* Then I would pull myself back to reality and whisper *You did it – you escaped.*

Patricia was good to me. She soon worked out that I had very little real experience of working with horses and that I was largely self-taught. As I said, riding was still painful due to the damage done through years of abuse, but it was good pain, pain I was willing to endure for the wonder of being closer to horses. Patricia was patient and taught me all she could about grooming and caring for the horses, as well as cleaning the stables and riding huge beasts. It was wonderful. There were other girls working there too – there was always quite a turnover – but, although I tried to be friendly, I also kept my distance. It was the horses I wanted and I was still wary of people.

I rarely strayed from the stables and never really socialised or ventured away from the paddocks or the small room I shared with three others. There was no need – everything I wanted was there.

Patricia ran the business with her partner, Lucas. He was a tall, handsome man who 'spoke posh'. Lucas was always around but never seemed to work as hard as Patricia. While she was happy to muck out, Lucas acted more as lord of the manor. I couldn't quite work out their relationship.

There was lots of gossip flying around about the two of them. Some rumours said that it was a marriage of convenience (they weren't actually married but were seen as that sort of couple in the community), others that Patricia was a lesbian. Whatever the truth of the situation I completely misread it. I was so wrapped up in the horses and in the fact that I had finally escaped from home that I didn't see what Lucas really was – another sexual predator. Only a few days after I arrived at the stables he cornered me as I was cleaning out.

'So,' he said sleazily, as I kept brushing the soiled hay out of the barn, 'Patricia tells me that you were very keen to join us here?'

I nodded and kept busy.

'Problems at home?' he asked.

'Sort of,' I muttered, not wanting to go into it at all.

'Boyfriend trouble I expect,' he said, edging closer.

I tried to back away but all that achieved was to leave me with nowhere to go, a wall behind me and Lucas in front.

'I wouldn't be at all surprised if you had all the boys running after you,' he went on, stroking my arm. 'Pretty young thing like you . . .'

I didn't think of myself as pretty and I certainly didn't have boys running after me. I had never wanted any of the male attention I had received and this man was acting just like all the others. He started touching me, telling me how lovely I was – but I suspected he had said it all many times before.

I did say no, I did say I didn't want this to happen, but I was a prime target really because, when push came to shove, I was conditioned to obey when any man pushed himself onto me. I'd been groomed into it, and even now, even as a young woman rather than a child, I felt that this was my role in life. Whenever a man wanted sex from me, that was what I was there for.

On top of that Lucas was one of my bosses. He made it clear that I was expected to do as he wanted and that I was to keep it from Patricia. As he put it, 'She wouldn't be interested – but she wouldn't want little gossips running around the stables either.'

A few days after his first attack on me one of the other girls started chatting to me as we worked.

'Has Lucas had a go yet?' she asked casually.

'What?' I replied, shocked that she would say such a thing.

'Well, if he hasn't, best prepare yourself,' she laughed. 'He thinks it's in our contracts – all the new girls have to get initiated!'

With that, she walked away. I was horrified. Was it really something to laugh about? Could it really be that when men took what they wanted it was nothing more than a joke?

Lucas soon lost interest. It didn't last for long, and when

another new girl started work he moved on to her. He was always perfectly friendly and pleasant towards me, as he was to all the girls, but in my eyes he was just another one on the long list of men who had taken advantage of and abused me.

Despite Lucas's actions Cornwall was so important for me. I started to realise who I was and what I was worth. I finally plucked up the courage to make trips home, and when I did I saw that I wasn't the only person who had changed.

Jed had a girlfriend, despite the fact that Granny had told me for years that this would never happen.

There was very little contact between any of them in Scotland and my mother. I started to write to her myself. She had visited a few times over the years but it had never gone well. I hoped that now I was an adult we could make our peace.

I knew that I couldn't stay in Cornwall for ever. It had been my escape, but it wasn't my home. On coming back I decided to adopt a certain persona to get me through. So, as soon as I returned, I set myself up as a witch, just like my granny. I exploited the reputation I had as someone with a heritage full of witches and a history of darkness, and I put about rumours that I had certain 'talents'. I didn't have to do much and it was laughable really, to see how easily fools like Jed would believe it all. It was the only time I believed he might be simple.

Any time I even saw him looking in my direction, I would hiss, 'Do you want me to light the black candle?'

I'd pretend to be getting up in order to go to the kitchen and get the candle which Granny had threatened people with for years and he would whimper, 'God, no, Sheena! No, please, no!'

Eventually I moved back to Scotland and everyone went on with their lives. I got a job working with horses again but made sure it was a long way from my family. My life changed yet again when I met a lad called Richard when I was working in some stables in Inverness. I loved him from the start – and never stopped loving him – but, to be honest, I was too badly scarred from everything that had happened to me in my past. I was living in a beautiful cottage in the old-fashioned stable-yard where I worked and Richard moved in with me soon after we met. The relationship never stood a chance. No one has ever taken his place in my heart, and I wonder whether we could have made a go of it if I'd had some help coming to terms with what had been done to me. As it was he gave me something so precious that I will always be grateful to him – our daughter.

When I became pregnant I couldn't work with the horses any more and, as a result, lost the house we had been staying in. I moved back near to my family and waited on the baby coming. It was a difficult time. I wanted this child so much, but the pregnancy threw up some awful memories for me. I felt so close to her from the start and couldn't help but go over, yet again, the thought process that had led my mum to abandon me.

I was pregnant when there was a knock at my door in the early hours of the morning. I knew that Jed's wife, Yvonne, had been taken into the maternity hospital in labour earlier that day, but I didn't think anyone would be bringing me news of her as it would be easier to phone at such an hour.

I was wrong.

Jed was standing there, visibly upset and hyperventilating.

I forgot all of our horrible past, worried for Yvonne and the baby.

'Jed – what's wrong?' I asked. 'What's happened?'

'It's the baby, Sheena,' he stuttered. 'The baby . . .'

My heart sank.

'Come in, Jed, come in.'

He staggered through the front door and found his way to my living room. I could hardly believe that I had invited him in, but I was worried about his wife and unborn child. I waited until he had composed himself enough to talk.

'It's a girl. Yvonne's had a wee lassie.'

'And – is there a problem?' I whispered, not really wanting to hear the answer if it was bad news.

'No, no,' he shook his head and I breathed a sigh of relief. 'It's just – she's just that perfect, Sheena. She's so beautiful and tiny . . . and . . .'

'And what?' I asked, fearing that there was something he wasn't telling me.

'Maria. That's what we've called her. Maria.'

'That's nice, Jed, that's nice,' I said.

'It's just – she's so perfect. I can't help thinking – I'll fucking kill anyone who lays a hand on her. If someone, if anyone, does that to her, I'll do them in. I'd do the dirty bastards in.'

Do *that*.

That's what he said, and he kept saying it, over and over again. He kept telling me how he would 'do in' anyone who did *that* to his new baby. *That*. What he did to me. It's what he meant, I'm sure of it.

He stayed there for ages, bawling his eyes out. I couldn't move. I had no idea how to respond. After a while he got up and moved towards me.

'Aw, Sheena,' he said, reaching out.

This was a step too far. I moved away, heading for the door without turning my back on him.

'No, Sheena – I'm not going to touch you, I'm not going to touch you.'

'I'd like you to leave now, Jed,' I said firmly.

'I'm not going to touch you, Sheena. It's just that wee lassie of mine – I'll kill anyone who goes near her, I swear I will.'

He rambled on for a while longer before finally leaving.

I sat in a chair in the dark, reflecting on what had just happened. Had he finally admitted what he had done to me was wrong? Had seeing his own newborn daughter finally shown to him the horror of his abuse of another vulnerable little girl all those years ago?

I don't know what he was thinking of that night, but I wasn't going to be the one to tell him all was forgiven.

Granny Morag was in her final days at that point, and I was pregnant and very emotional. Despite how horrible she had been to me she was still my granny. I had always loved her deep down and wanted her to love me, and she was an old, lonely woman. The badness was finished for me. She couldn't touch me any more. If I allowed memories of me and my mum, of how she had sent my dad away, of how she had never protected me from abuse, to fill my mind, I would never have been able to move on.

By this stage she was on a lot of morphine and talking more than I had ever known.

'You know I had two babies before your mother?' she asked one night as I sat with her.

I nodded.

'You know what happened?' she continued. Without waiting for an answer, she went on. 'They killed my babies, you know. My two boys. I had my first baby and they took him away. Then they sent *me* away, Sheena. They sent me to the asylum and they put me in a padded cell. They wanted to break me.'

As the tears rolled down her old cheeks I realised I had never seen her cry before.

'They wanted to break me,' she repeated. A dry, hollow laugh came from her. 'They already had. When they took my baby away and never even let me hold him, they broke me then.'

'What did they do to you?' I whispered.

Her eyes were closed but her voice was strong. 'They put me in the padded cell and the only other thing in there was a potty. I was in a padded cell because they wanted people to think I was mad. If I was mad, that was an excuse – an excuse for me being pregnant and unwed. So, they would have less shame. They'd rather have people think I was a lunatic than have me safe and happy with a bastard baby.' A wry smile crept over her thin lips. 'So . . . I gave them mad. I took my clothes off, stripped naked as the day I was born, put the potty on my head and did the cancan!'

She stopped smiling.

'My father came to see me, to tell me that my baby was dead. My little Jed.'

I shivered at the mention of his name and Granny must have noticed the look on my face.

'Aye,' she said, 'I named your uncle for my poor, dead boy, my firstborn.'

'What happened next?' I asked.

'I was a good girl. I was a good girl for two years, then they let me out. I went back to my loving family – my loving family who had killed my baby, I'm sure of it, and I did it again. I got pregnant again. And, again, there was no ring on my finger. They threatened me, especially my father, and he said he'd put me in the madhouse, but I told him I'd scream from the rooftops about what he'd done to my wee Jed if he even tried it. So, they kept me inside until it was my time. Then when I birthed that baby, they took him away too. I was left in a room on my own, my body crying out for my bairn until my father came back in and said that one was dead too.

'I knew better next time,' she said. 'I knew that I needed a man and a ring on my finger. So I married your Granddad – your real Granddad, your mum's dad. He was my first husband and he was a good man but I just wanted a bairn, Sheena. I just wanted a bairn.'

'You had Mum first?' I asked, even although I knew she had.

'Aye. I wanted a boy, I'll admit it. I wanted a boy to try and fill the hole left by the two I'd never held.'

I was very surprised that she was telling me things but even more so that she was being so emotional about it. I had always characterised my granny as a hard woman – and she was – but this peek into her world, the world she had lived in as a young girl, was a revelation to me. It was inconceivable that these losses wouldn't have marked her. Experiences like that affect people, women, so strongly and they never go away. To lose two children and be betrayed by her own father must have been devastating. Yes, she was hard and unemotional, but she must have learned that and she must have been incredibly strong to get through it all.

It was no excuse for what she had done, and allowed to be done, to me, but it was still an insight into how Granny's own character had been shaped.

As I left her I reached over the bed to hug her. She squirmed in my arms.

'That's enough of that bloody nonsense,' she said.

'I love you, Granny,' I said, ignoring her harsh tone. She was unused to showing or receiving affection but I hoped that this moment would be a breakthrough in our relationship. I placed a tender kiss on her dry cheek, but she pushed me away.

'I mean it – piss off with all that nonsense. Now, leave me to sleep,' she commanded. She closed her eyes defiantly, warding off any further attempts at affection. She needn't have worried. I'd had my wrists slapped – yet again.

When I returned a few days later she was back to her usual cranky self and still trying to hurt people by revealing things from the past. That day, as the wind howled outside the cottage, and the shadows played on the walls of the room I had crept into for so many years, stealing biscuits and trying to hide, she told me about sending my father away. I had already heard of that from one of my uncles, but had never known how much he was saying out of spite. I had been incredulous that they could all have so willingly and deliberately ruined Mum's life and I probably didn't want to believe it. However, Granny Morag confirmed it all on her deathbed. I didn't have to drag anything out of her and I never raised the topic; she seemed proud of what she had done.

'I sent your father on his way, you know,' she wheezed one day.

'What do you mean?' I asked, wanting to hear the story from her.

'You've never to repeat a word of this to Kathleen but – well, it was me. I got rid of him.' A smile crept across her lips as she remembered.

'What did you do, Granny?'

'Brian. That was his name. Brian. D'you know anything about him?' she enquired.

I made a non-committal noise, but she barely paused before continuing the story.

'Your mother was daft about him. She had a belly full of bastard and her head in the clouds. Oh, she was sure he was going to marry her; she thought he'd come back and make everything perfect, but I knew better. I got his name and met him in Edinburgh. Me and two of your uncles went and put him in the picture.'

It was horrific. Mum hadn't known back then that her own mother had rifled through her things many months earlier and found Brian's details. She had contacted him and discovered that he was back in Edinburgh. She arranged to meet him, pretending that she had news of Kathleen, but instead went to the station with two of her sons to threaten him. Brian was told that if he ever attempted to make any contact with Kathleen, he wouldn't live to tell the tale. When he said it would take more than that to prevent him from finding out about the love of his life and his baby, Granny Morag broke his heart.

'You're stupid as well as deluded,' she had said. 'You're history. Kathleen's never been shy with the boys – even if you are the wee bastard's father, which is highly unlikely, she's moved on. She's married to someone else and that poor fool thinks he's the dad. So bugger off and never let me see your face again.'

He left – for ever.

Granny was now laughingly telling me the details, as if it was all a funny joke rather than evidence of a twisted family who had shattered the dreams of not just Mum, but mine too.

When Granny asked Mum for details of Brian, she had already discovered that his own father – who shared the same Christian name and very unusual surname – had also been in the Australian Navy and had been killed in action. It was a letter confirming that death which she showed to her own daughter, revelling in the pain she caused.

It was a horrible thing to do to your own daughter, and what strikes me now as much as when I first heard the story, is that it was for nothing. Granny Morag wasn't protecting Mum from a man who didn't love her or who would break her heart, she was keeping a young couple apart who were intent on being together. Dad *did* plan to come for her and they were going to raise me together. Granny put an end to all of that and she did so in a way which left no loose threads. Brian was left with questions over my paternity – which was a complete lie as my mother had never been with anyone else – and a belief that the love of his life had fallen for someone else. And my mum? She believed the father of her child was dead. There was no going back for either of them, nothing for them to chase, because they had both been persuaded by one wicked old woman that it was all over.

She laughed to herself.

'Do you know what the funny thing was?'

I shook my head.

'He *was* going to marry her! He had planned to come back, put a ring on her finger and give you his name. He was just as daft as her. He thought they'd make a lovely wee family together and sail off into the sunset. How stupid was that?' she snorted.

'It doesn't sound stupid to me,' I ventured.

'Well, it fucking was,' she declared. 'A stupid idea. Kathleen would have gone!'

'But she did go, Granny,' I reminded her. 'She did go.'

'She didn't go with him,' she stated.

Was that what it was all about? Had she deliberately ruined her own daughter's life just to have some sense of control? I could barely think of what had been lost. While Mum had met someone else and had gone on to have her American family with a wonderful life, I felt as if my own life had been snatched away from me by this wicked old woman who had thought of nothing more than her own needs.

'Is that all that mattered to you?' I demanded. 'Did you just want to be the one pulling the strings? Did it not matter to you who was hurt?'

'Don't be so bloody melodramatic!' she snapped. 'No one was

hurt. Your mother pissed off to America anyway, she couldn't wait to get shot of you. I was the one who had to bring you up, and it wasn't easy. You were a little liar from the day you were born – we all know that.'

'I was NOT a liar!' I shouted. 'I was hurt, Gran. You know that. Eddie hurt me and Jed hurt me. That would never have happened if Mum and Dad had married, if they had raised me.'

'Well, it never happened anyway, did it?' she said. 'Not the way you go on about it. We all know what you are, Sheena; we all know what you always were. A liar. A lassie who couldn't keep her knickers on. A lassie who would do anything for a sweetie.'

'At four? At six? At eight and nine and ten?' I screamed. 'Really? It was all my fault?'

'Aye. Aye, it was. You need to move on,' she said.

'From being abused? How do I do that, exactly? I'd love to know.' All of the fight had gone out of me and there was no screaming left.

'This is all very heartless of you,' she said. 'I'm an old woman, I can do without this. My Jed isn't right, you know, he's not right in the head. Poor laddie. He needed a woman, and he was always careful with you. He had those French letters, you were never going to have a bairn now, were you?'

I could hardly believe what I was hearing.

Was she really saying that raping a child was fine as long as contraception was used? Was she still claiming that 'poor' Jed was so simple that I was helping out by letting him abuse me?

'Anyway . . . that doesn't matter,' she decided. 'I don't want you telling Kathleen what I've just said to you about your dad. She doesn't need to know any of this.'

Granny was a wicked old woman. All she cared about was what she thought was best, with never any concern for other people.

'I don't understand you,' I said. 'You've had a hard life – you've lost babies, you've been treated badly. So, why do the same to other people?'

'A hard life? Me?' She laughed weakly. 'You don't know the half of it, Sheena. Men. That's the problem. I've been telling you that since you could listen. What my father did to me was heartless. When he sent me away, when he killed my babies – because, by Christ, I know that's what he did – he made sure that I'd never trust anyone ever again.'

'But you must have loved your other children?' I asked.

'Aye – aye, I did, but being soft helps no one. Your mother needed direction.'

'But she left, she left!' I said again. 'You didn't get to keep her once she had me anyway, she went to America.'

'More fool her. If she'd stayed here, I'd have looked after her.'

'She had a life! She had a family and a good man in America – she didn't need you, did she?' I reminded her. Perhaps I was being cruel by saying these things, but this old woman had never shied away from cruelty herself.

'She didn't leave me,' she snarled. 'She left *you*. She'd have stayed if it wasn't for you . . .'

'No!' I couldn't bear this. 'She loved me! She left because of you!'

'No mother leaves a child she loves. A mother always stands by her own.'

'Like you stand by Jed?' I countered.

She stared at me. I couldn't tell whether she hated me or loved me.

'Aye. Just like I stand by Jed. Your mother left you, deserted you. I was more of a mother to you than she ever was, and don't you forget it.'

'How could I? How could I forget it, when your "mothering" sent me straight to hell?' I asked.

'Face up to the facts, Sheena – Kathleen wouldn't have left if it wasn't for you. You were holding her back. If she'd wanted you, she wouldn't have signed you away to me. You were a bastard and she had plans. Her fancy new man wouldn't want you in their perfect life, would he? She had plenty of other bairns – you were the only one she dumped. Ask yourself why, go on. Maybe . . . maybe . . .' Her voice tailed off, but I knew that she had plenty more to say, despite her physical weakness.

'Maybe what?' I knew I should leave it, I knew she would only hurt me more, but Granny Morag was dying and I might never have another chance to have all of this out with her again.

'Maybe she knew you were bad inside.'

I was shocked. This was the worst thing she could say to me. Granny had thrown some hurtful comments at me over the years, but this was horrible.

'Maybe she knew that you wouldn't just drag her down, but that you would poison things. The way you were with Jed – what if you'd been like that with her new man? What if you'd been like that with your half-brothers? Christ, you'd do anything for sweeties – what would you have been like in America? You were always a dirty little bitch, Sheena.'

'How can you say these things?' I asked her, the tears springing to my eyes yet again. 'How can you hurt me when you say you were a mother to me?'

'I WAS a fucking mother to you!' She had more power in her voice at that point than I had heard from her in months. 'I raised you, I clothed you, I fed you . . .'

'You were paid for it all,' I interrupted. 'My mother clothed me. You did nothing to keep me safe. You got money from social services and you lied to them about everything. It was all a charade. You sit there and ask me to keep the truth from my own mum? I'm sure she knows all about you – after all, if you had been a decent mother to her in the first place, she would have felt that she could stay here and raise me, not go to the other side of the world to get away from you.'

I knew these were harsh words, a low blow to a dying woman, but Granny Morag was right in one sense; she *had* raised me, and she had raised me never to mince my words or have any concern for the feelings of others. I hadn't been like that – until now.

'Get out of my sight!' she hissed. 'You're an ungrateful little bitch. A slut and a whore, just like Kathleen. I don't know why I ever bothered with you. Get out and don't come back!'

She got her wish.

I left and I never saw her again.

Two days after that encounter, I got the news from Auntie

Betty that Granny had died. She had been riddled with cancer and emphysema, and had finally left this world bitter and alone. No one was with her when she took her last breath. She was lying in her bedroom alone, having been just as horrible to almost everyone else in her final days as she was to me. The only person she had a civil word for was Jed, as always, and he'd been too busy to spend time with the mother who adored him and who had covered for him, making excuses for her own perverted son for decades.

Chapter 21

Goodbye

When Granny Morag died, it set something free. I could be myself. I had three children and I did what I could to move on from my past. As soon as my first daughter, Cathy, was born I made a promise to her and myself – I would never mistreat her and I would always be there for her, and it was a promise I made to each baby in turn.

I kept some things, some habits, from my childhood – I devoured books and retained my love of animals, but there was one thing that still needed to be resolved: my relationship with Mum.

Over a difficult thirty years we made our peace. I met with my American brothers and sisters, and I came to think of my mum's husband as my father. They were good people and we all had a lot of questions. I guess that they were as much in the dark about some things too. Their mother had this whole life that they knew very little of – and I knew that if I told them what had gone on I would be opening up a whole world of horror for them. They were related to Jed, they were related to Betty, we had the same maternal grandmother – and I could blow their worlds apart by sharing my story with them.

It wasn't something I could do immediately – and, in fact, it hasn't been something I've been able to do completely until now. They all welcomed me into their families with love and affection. I was humbled by them in many ways. All of them had achieved so much with their lives, and I felt that I was worthless in comparison. They never did anything to make me feel that way, it was simply my own lack of self-worth yet again.

As time went on Mum and I would sometimes talk about what had gone on, but it was hard. I never told her the whole story. How could I? How could I put all of that onto her? Instead, we worked on the love we had for each other, the pure side of our bond, untouched by anyone else. She told me that she'd made many visits when I was little but had never been allowed to the house. On the occasion I do remember her coming, she had organised everything herself, whereas in the past she had given warning so that one of her brothers would be there to pick her up from the airport, and this had allowed Morag to head her off at the pass. We made plans – plans to quilt together, plans to travel together, plans to spend time together without dwelling on the past.

I was at work one night when I got the call.

It was my son, Alan.

'Mum,' he said gently, 'this is going to come as a terrible shock, but I've got bad news for you . . .'

'It's my mum, isn't it?' I said instantly.

I just knew.

The tone of his voice, the longing in my heart for her – I just knew.

'Oh, Mum,' he said. 'It is. I'm so sorry. There's just been a message from your brother – Nana's gone.'

I panicked.

I felt that I was going to stop breathing, that my chest was being pushed by a heavy weight, that everything was spinning. I was hyperventilating and calling 'Mum, Mum!' over and over again.

Alan was still on the phone and he was listening to all of this. I was all alone at work and he was scared by what he heard.

'Mum!' I could hear him shouting, 'Mum! I'm coming to get you! Don't do anything, just wait for me!'

He hung up and I pushed the phone into my pocket. I walked outside and just started to scream. The place where I work is isolated, miles away from anything, and no one could hear me. It was dark and it was cold, but all I could feel was my pain.

Mum was gone.

Gone.

Gone.

Gone.

And this time, it was for ever.

I remember what I screamed.

They've taken my mum, they've taken my mum, I cried, over and over.

That was what it felt like. It felt as if some power, some power greater than me, had taken her away from me again, just as they had when I was a little girl. This was a punishment for something,

I was sure of it. We had so much still to do together, so much love to share, and it had all been snatched away.

I couldn't stop screaming. I hadn't screamed since Eddie raped me in those toilets all those years ago. I let it all out, then bit my lip. I was distraught but I had learned, long ago, that keeping emotions inside was expected of me. My son was coming and when he arrived I would not be a gibbering wreck.

It was so hard. Even when Alan was there, I felt completely alone. In fact, I felt like a wee girl again. Mum and I had just started to really get to know each other. We had been discussing going to craft fairs together and we were both making memory quilts. She had been planning to come to Scotland with her husband the next summer and we were going to have a wonderful, indulgent time together.

And now – now I felt as if my past had taken her away.

Alan took me home and the rest of that night passed in a haze. I wasn't feeling anything different to millions of other people who lose their mums, but I was finding it hard to separate the loss of her the first time from the loss now. All I knew was that I desperately wanted to go to Mum's funeral but I had no money. Not a penny. I'd always scrimped and saved to get through life and I'd never resented it, not really. I always clung on to the fact that there were things so much more important than material goods and cash. I focused on love and my children, on what I could give them that cost nothing, but now that I was actually being prevented from saying goodbye to Mum, it cut me like a knife. There was nowhere to turn. My children weren't rich and they had their own responsibilities to think of. I had no savings and nothing of value to sell.

There was only one person I knew with money. One person who always had spare cash. One person who I thought I would never have to be in touch with again.

Jed.

I knew he had the means, but could I bring myself to ask him?

My mind wouldn't settle and my stomach churned. Going to Mum's funeral meant so much to me. It would give me a final chance to say some things to her that needed to be said – even if she was only there in spirit to hear them. Perhaps some people won't understand what I was feeling and it *is* hard to explain; however, the thought that my mum might be surrounded by her American family as they laid her to rest, without me, without her firstborn, ripped the heart from me. I needed to be there.

And so I did it.

I contacted Jed.

My hands were shaking so much that I could hardly dial the number. I started and gave up half-a-dozen times, always stopping myself from pressing the last digit to connect me to the man who had made my childhood a living hell. I was having flashbacks, sweating. I was in a panic, terrified about opening up any contact with him again, but also recognising that he was my only hope. He could make this all possible.

Finally, I did it.

Each ring of the phone felt like it was going on for ever. I didn't know what would be worse – if he did pick up and I had to speak to him, or if he didn't and I had to go through all of this again.

Just as I was telling myself that he wasn't there, a gruff voice said, 'Hello?'

Him.

Jed.

I froze and couldn't say a word.

'Hello? Hello?' he repeated. 'Who's there? What d'you want?' he asked.

'Jed?' I whispered.

'Aye, it's Jed – who's this?' he asked.

'Sheena. It's Sheena,' I said quietly.

'Sheena?' He paused, then laughed. 'Sheena? Our Sheena?'

I wasn't his. I wasn't anything to do with him. This was all about me trying to get to my mum and, while I would do all I could to make that happen, I felt sick even talking to him.

'Yes, it's Sheena, Jed – have you heard about my mum?'

'Aye, I heard – what about it?'

'She was your sister, Jed; surely that means something?' I asked.

'Not really. She made her choices a long time ago. We were nothing to her. She had her own life, with her big fancy American house and all that money.'

I could tell that Jed had made his mind up a long time ago about my mum. In his mind, the very fact that she had made something of herself all came down to money and what he assumed her life must have been like.

'So – she left you a fortune then?' he went on.

'No . . . I don't know. She isn't even buried yet, Jed. I'm not thinking about anything like that.'

'Aye, well – she had plenty of bairns to that Yankee fella, didn't she? I doubt she'll remember to leave you anything.'

I swallowed hard and tried to find the courage for what I needed to ask this loathsome man.

'Jed – I need your help with something,' I began.

'Oh, do you now?' he chortled. 'Do you now? Well, that's interesting, Sheena, that's very, very interesting. What could you possibly want from me?'

'It's Mum. It's about her funeral. I really want to go to it . . .' I stammered.

'Well, off you go then,' he interrupted, 'you don't need my blessing. Have a nice time. Bye.'

'No, Jed, wait!' I shouted into the phone. 'It's . . . well . . . I—'

'Spit it out, girl,' he snapped.

'I can't afford it, Jed. I can't afford to go to America and say goodbye to Mum.'

'So?' he snarled. 'What do you expect me to do about it?'

I closed my eyes and prepared to beg. 'I hoped you would lend me the money, Jed.'

Silence.

'I wouldn't ask unless I was desperate, you know that. I've nowhere to turn, no one to ask – except you.'

'You want money from me?' he replied.

'Yes. Please. It would just be a loan. I'd get the cheapest flight possible, and I'll pay you back as soon as I can. I know you have money, Jed, I know that you got a pay-off from work and you've always had savings. Please. I'm begging you.'

'Are you? Are you begging me, Sheena?'

I knew that he was smiling. I could hear it, ridiculous though that may sound.

'I am,' I answered with tears falling down my cheeks. I'd lost my mum and now I was losing any shred of dignity I had.

'Why would I give you money, Sheena?'

'To help me out, Jed. To help me go to my mum.'

'And why would I want to help you out?' he asked again.

I hadn't wanted to say it, I hadn't wanted to speak the words that would make us both realise what he owed me, but he was pushing me to.

'You know what you did to me, Jed,' I said, trying to squeeze out some bravery from somewhere. 'You alone know just what you did to me when I was a child. You can never make up for that, but this, this is your chance to help me for once. Please.'

'You want me to give you money because of what happened?' he hissed.

'Yes. Yes I do.'

He paused.

'You had plenty of money from me, you dirty little bitch. Every time you got me to do what you wanted, you somehow managed to make me pay for it as well. Have you forgotten all the times I gave you money when you were wee? Now you still want to bleed me dry? That takes some beating, it really does.'

'What?' I wept. 'What?'

'You've been paid. You've been paid plenty. Anything that happened back then was because you wanted it and if you ever, *ever* think you can tell anyone about it, just you remember what

I'll tell them about *you*. You wanted money. You wanted sweet-ies. You knew what you were doing.'

'I was a child, Jed, a child. You were the one who made me do all those things, who did all of those things *to* me. Will you help me now, will you?'

'Will I hell,' he said, and with that he slammed the phone down.

I know it may seem odd that I didn't ask Robbie or Freddie for the money for the flight. After all, they had always been kind and generous to me, whereas Jed had done nothing but bring trouble and fear into my life. All I can say is that, at the moment when I knew I had lost my mum, I desperately wanted my life to be different. She was what I wanted more than anything, of course, but I also needed closure on my childhood. When I made that choice to call Jed, there was a part of me that desperately hoped he would apologise for all he had done and offer me the money without strings. If he had done that, something would have come out of mum's passing. I think all abuse survivors want to rewrite their childhoods and there was a, very naive, part of me that day which felt this was an opportunity to do just that. I'm not a bitter person. If Jed had admitted he had been wrong, and if he had seemed genuinely contrite, I could have moved past it. I should have known better.

His reaction cut me like a knife. In the middle of grieving for my mum and trying to find the money to go to her funeral, I was faced with this too. His words forced me to look at something which I had avoided for years but which now kept going through my mind – did I want to do anything about this? *Did I want to tell the police what Jed had done?*

It isn't a decision which can be made lightly by anyone. I knew that there would be huge repercussions if I did decide to go to the police, but I was also furious at what he had said. Perhaps my grief was making things worse, but his refusal to help me out financially so that I could go to Mum's funeral hurt so much.

I had never wanted to ask this man for anything, but I had nowhere else to turn. His response – that I had traded sex for money – horrified me, but it also made me ashamed. Was he right? Is that what happened? Had it been nothing more than a transaction?

I lay awake in bed that night with everything rushing about in my head. My mum was dead, and I needed to grieve – I also needed to get my trip organised and find the money from somewhere – but Jed's words had taken over. I couldn't move past what he had said to me. Was it my fault? I couldn't stop thinking about what had been done to me as a child, by Jed and by Eddie. Eddie wasn't someone who would stop anything voluntarily and he had raped me anally about a dozen times after that first occasion. The thing which sticks with me now is that I know I was never quiet. I *always* screamed. He would tell me not to, he would tell me to shut up, but the pain was excruciating, I never got used to it, and it was a natural reaction to scream as loudly as I could. Each time I could hear people outside walking past and never, not on one single occasion, did anyone ever come in to see why a child was screaming in the men's public toilets. What did they think was going on? I was screaming blue murder and shouting at him to stop and yet no one ever thought to investigate? Sometimes I have wondered whether Eddie had positioned someone outside to stand guard as it were, someone who had the same tendencies as him, but that doesn't seem possible. I never saw anyone and he never sent me to anyone else, so I think it was just a combination of him being lucky and people being used to keeping their noses out of other people's business in those days. How could that all be explained as 'my fault'? Jed was piling the guilt on me and it was making me play everything over in my mind again. Yet there were things I couldn't take responsibility for, no matter how much I hated myself.

On top of this I knew that Eddie had abused others too – it wasn't just me and, therefore, it was something which was rotten in *him*. Celia had told me that he had abused her too. Not only that, but as a result of being raped she had actually borne him a child – a child to her own brother – who was given up for adoption. This had happened long before I got to know the Johnstones; long before Betty married Charlie, but it was the history on which they were built. Secrets and lies and perversions were just ordinary things to them. Once I discovered what Celia had been through I had a clearer picture of the ways in which Eddie had been allowed to get away with things, especially by his sisters. Jed's words were throwing me back into the past, making me question myself and wonder whether I had done enough to get out of it – could I have made Betty listen? Was there anyone I could have told?

I didn't know what to believe. I wasn't sure. I was so confused and hurting so much that I could barely think straight. All I knew was that I had to get to America, and no one here would help me. I called Betty, who I had previously told about Jed's attacks on me, the one who had been responsible for it all starting with her brother-in-law all those years ago.

'Betty,' I said, 'I spoke to Jed. I need some money to go to Mum's funeral. I don't have a penny and he won't give it to me,' I wept. 'I just want to say goodbye to Mum, I need to be there.'

'Why should he give you money?' she asked, not a shred of emotion in her voice, despite the fact that it was her own sister we were talking about.

'You know what he did to me, Betty,' I said. 'He owes me.'

'I know what you *said* he did to you,' she retorted. 'He owes you nothing.'

'What?' I whispered. 'Can you still deny it after all these years? Can you still deny that he abused me?'

I heard her sigh. 'I can't believe that you're still at it,' she said.

'At it?' I repeated.

'Aye. Picking away at this like a scab. You know what, Sheena? You're lucky no one's ever put you in jail for what you say about Jed. We all know what happened there,' she sniffed.

'What? What do you think happened, Betty?' I asked.

'Well, you were always after him – you must have made it hard for him to keep away,' she snapped.

'When I was a child?' I asked, bewildered. 'You think that a child can . . . what? . . . *lure* a grown man into abusing her?'

'You're trying to make me feel guilty. It wasn't abuse, Sheena, you know that full well. You were always old for your age.'

'I was nine, Betty. I was nine.'

'So? You need to get over it. He owes you nothing, and you need to just move on.'

She put the phone down on me. I was in shock. It was just one thing after another, and no one — no one at all — seemed to be affected by Mum's death one bit.

I started phoning around, finding out about emergency loans, seeing where I could get money at short notice — of course, they were all loan sharks, but I couldn't see where else to turn. Then, out of the blue, my half-sister Marilyn called from America.

'Have you got your flights booked yet, Sheena?' she asked.

I hesitated, my pride preventing me from admitting the truth. 'Well . . .' I began.

'The thing is, Sheena,' she interrupted, 'we really don't want you to feel bad about this or think that we're patronising you but you're family, sweetheart, and we all want you there. Mum would want you there, she'd want us all together so — just book a flight and we'll pay for it. Just get here, Sheena — please just get here so we can be together.'

The relief was overwhelming. Within twenty-four hours I was on my way. There had been no further contact with Jed and, to be honest, even if he had offered me the money after thinking about it I would have found another way. His words had hurt me so much and taken me back to a place I never wanted to revisit, especially at a time like this.

When I got to America I was immediately taken into the heart of my 'other' family. All of my half-brothers and half-sisters were there and we grieved together for the woman we had lost. I felt part of it, I felt part of that family, but I knew that I had a different story with different questions which would now always remain unanswered.

I pieced together Mum's last moments from what my American family told me. Her health hadn't been too good in the last few years – she'd suffered a heart aneurysm five years earlier – but she kept busy and she did take part in lots of activities. On her last morning she told her husband, Bob, that she felt she was coming down with flu. 'She had aches all over,' Bob told me, 'and she was exhausted.' Mum said that she just needed a rest and encouraged Bob to go to the gym, which he did. 'She said that she'd be better when I got back, that she just needed a little time to recharge her batteries. I had no idea,' he told me, his eyes full of tears as he recounted the final time they spoke to each other.

When he got back from the gym Mum was lying on the floor. She'd had a massive heart attack. He called 911 and the paramedics tried to revive her, but it was too late, she'd passed away.

Throughout the time before the funeral, at the service, and immediately afterwards, I felt completely lost, even though people were terribly kind. The whole visit broke me in two and I genuinely didn't think it would hurt as much. I've lost people before, of course I have and, like anyone, I know the emotional impact of death but this . . . this was different to anything I'd ever experienced.

What I tried to do was immerse myself in Mum's life. I spoke to everyone I could, I absorbed everything I could. The one thing which stood out was the way in which all of her friends tried to reassure me about how much she had loved me. I was told, on many occasions, of how she had worked at two jobs, as had my stepfather, to get the money together for a legal battle to try and get me back. They had both tried. Lawyers had been consulted, steps had been taken, but the cost of an international custody battle was phenomenal, especially given that Mum had apparently voluntarily signed me over to Granny Morag. Of course, knowing what I knew, I was fully aware of what that 'voluntary' action might have really involved but, on paper, and from a legal perspective, Mum and her husband had very little leverage. Every letter from an American lawyer, every phone call, every visit, cost a fortune. When I was eleven, she had, apparently, finally listened and decided she had to accept that I wasn't coming back to her – not until I could make my own choices, that is. In fact, I was told that one lawyer had specifically said: 'Leave it, Kathleen – she'll come for you.'

I was consumed with guilt that I never had. Mum had been all those miles away, wanting me, yet I had never gone to her. I could have. If I had really tried, I could have gone when I first left home. It would have been close to impossible once I had my own children as I could never leave them, but there *had* been a window of opportunity and I hadn't taken it. The truth was, I had wasted my time hating Mum for years. I had been so upset that she had never swooped into my life, rescued me and carried me off to America that I had never taken the initiative and changed things once I was old enough to do so. All of that time could never be brought back – I cursed every bad thought I'd had, every moment I'd blamed her rather than just realising that she meant the world to me. Now I was faced with the reality that I had meant the world to her too.

'She never stopped talking about you, her daughter in Scotland,' one woman told me at the funeral.

Another came up to me and took me in her arms. 'I'm so glad to have finally have met Kathleen's little girl,' she said.

It didn't stop. So many people knew who I was and I spent three days being told how much Mum had loved me, how she had fought for me, and how she had always hoped that she would have me back one day. However, in the end she had to give up the legal fight – it was costing too much, going nowhere, and she had her other children to think of. One of my half-brothers, Sean, had major health problems and as there's no NHS in the States the medical bills for him were horrendous.

After the funeral I sat down with my American family and we had a good chat. I found out so many things from them.

'Mum always hoped that you'd come here to be with her,' revealed Frances. 'She told me quite recently that she thought you would fly out as soon as you were old enough to get away from Granny Morag. I think she often wondered why that didn't happen.'

What could I tell them? Of course, now, I was heartbroken at the thought of the life I'd missed, but I had been raised to hate Mum for abandoning me, so the idea of simply jetting off to her open arms when I had turned eighteen had seemed laughable. I was also faced with a dilemma about how much I should tell Frances and the others. Granny Morag was their maternal grandmother too, and anything I revealed about what she had done to me and allowed to be done to me would have an impact on how they perceived a member of their own family. To be honest, I also wondered what they would think of me if they knew what Jed and the others had done – would they think less of me, think I was damaged goods, think I was less worthy of being part of their family?

There was so much to consider. If I opened this door they would know that their aunt had allowed me to be abused when I was little more than a toddler, that their uncle had then abused me until I was a teenager, that their grandmother had allowed it all to go on, and that their own mother had left me to that fate. I wasn't just facing my demons – I was facing the possibility of tarnishing their memories and making them hate me in the process.

I said nothing. It was what I had been trained to do, and I could still do it when I had to.

So I grieved with them, but I also grieved alone.

On the flight back, I thought about what had happened. I had started to write this book just before Mum died, so I had been thinking about my life more in those few months than in all of the previous decades, but that flight home to Scotland made me flick back over the years in a strange bubble of loneliness and reflection.

Every memory brought another. Every time I thought I had a clear image of me at one stage of myself, another image from earlier came into focus. It was as if I was looking at mental photographs of myself, and there was always another layer.

I thought of myself at eighteen. I had wanted to teach and maybe I would have managed that if Mum had been around. English and reading books had saved me so many times, and I had dreamed of being able to bring that magic into the lives of other people too, but it had never happened.

I know now that Mum had kept hoping that I would come to

her in America as soon as I was old enough. I had been raised to hate her for 'abandoning' me, but if only I had challenged that both of our lives could have been so different. I wish I could turn back the clock. After she died I tried to access my social work records to try and make sense of so many things. I thought that there might be some clues in there – I guess what I really hoped was that someone somewhere had perhaps noticed that not everything was right. I wanted to feel that someone had cared. Had questions been asked about how I was raised? Did anyone think that Granny Morag was putting on a front when the social workers came round?

It wasn't to be. I was told all of the documents had been destroyed when I turned forty, almost twenty years ago. I did get a lawyer involved but as that brought no joy either I can only assume they're telling the truth and there's nothing left.

I then tried to get to see my medical records but, again, was thwarted. Everything from the time I was born to when I turned eighteen is 'missing'. I currently have a doctor attempting to access them for me as I've been told they might still be in storage somewhere.

It's taking such a long time to put the pieces of my own life together. I'll never get the answers to many of my questions. The sad truth is that there's no one left to answer them.

The whole issue of fault and who was to blame had always been at the heart of this. Granny Morag had always said Jed wasn't to blame. Jed himself had always said it wasn't his fault. And I had never really questioned it when they said these things . . . until I was writing this book. When I told someone who was helping me that it wasn't Jed's fault (and I believed the line they had all been feeding me for years), she stopped me in my tracks by saying, 'Well, if it wasn't Jed's fault, whose fault was it?'

'What do you mean?' I asked.

'When he raped you – there was you, and there was him. If it wasn't his fault, whose fault was it? Who does it leave if you believe that?'

'Me,' I whispered. 'It was my fault.'

'Really?' she went on. 'You think that a child is to blame for being raped? You think you were to blame for what he did to you? Would you think that of any other child if you were listening to this story and it wasn't your own life?'

No!

Of course I wouldn't. I would tell that child that the adult was to blame, that the adult made their own choices. I would tell that child that they should have been protected and that it wasn't their fault. And yet I had believed the lies of Jed and Granny Morag for years when they told me that it was all down to me. Why could I not see what had been staring me in the face all this time? Why could I not see that Jed was responsible for his own actions?

I had always been led to believe that Jed was 'simple'. Yet when I started talking about my life I could see what I had closed my eyes to for decades.

If he was so simple, how had he managed to keep a job all his life?

If he was so simple, how had he managed to marry, make a home, have children, and keep his life together?

He'd never been sacked or made homeless; he'd never been

sectioned or committed to any sort of psychiatric care. He'd had a normal life – I was the one paying the price for his 'problems'.

I always have, I guess. I've always paid the price for everyone else.

When you are abused there are times when you can push it away. As an adult I tried to make a life for myself, and I succeeded against the odds, but every so often my past crept in. You can't think about the abuse every second of every day or you would go mad. However, it does leave a mark. Even if you can't see the scars, they're still there.

When I look at my own granddaughter at the age I was when Eddie started abusing me, it breaks me in two. She's so tiny, so vulnerable. I can't even imagine how her body would take such things, never mind her heart.

My children mean the world to me and that is what I will never understand – how could I have been left behind? How could my mother have done that?

However, I need to focus on the future. I need to focus on what I have, not what I've lost. I have my children, my grand-children, and my faith. I have my story written down in black and white.

I have myself.

I'm not waiting on anyone to rescue me any more.

I can do that myself.

And I will.

I will, Mum.

Epilogue

Dear Mum –
It's been a little while since you went away; since you went away *again*. I can't stop thinking about you and I can't shake the feeling that this is the second time I've lost you. I wonder how much pain I can take?

I can't stop thinking about you. I have so many questions and they'll never be answered now that you've died. I feel as if there will always be a huge gap in my life, not just because you've gone, but because the answers have gone too. No one but you could ever have helped me find the missing pieces of the jigsaw which is my life, and now, I'll never know the truth.

I was so proud of you, Mum, but I know I never showed it because I thought you hated me and were ashamed of me. Was there any truth in that, Mum? When you met my stepfather, you must have felt some shame, because you did have a child out of wedlock, which meant something back then, and he was from a religious family, so they would have been shocked. Did you ever get over that shame? Did you ever wish me away, wish that your life and being a mother had started when you went to America, rather than with me?

Granny Morag always said that you put your other children first. Although I know she could be a wicked woman, her words stick in my mind. Why did you pay for them to come on holiday back to Scotland, but hardly gave me any time alone with you? Why did you never take me back with you? Why did you spend the money on bringing them here, rather than sending a ticket for me to come and live with you? That hurts and it always will. It hurts that they have such good lives, and I still carry the burden of what was done to me when you left. Even if I had still been abused, even if you hadn't taken me back until I was a young woman, perhaps, with your love and help and support, I could have moved past all of this better. It wouldn't still be eating away at me.

I have no idea what you really felt for me. I could never leave any of my children – which is why, when I was older, I didn't just pack my bags and run to you. How did you do it, Mum? How did you live with yourself knowing there was a little girl crying herself to sleep while you had more babies and hugged *them* tight? I just want to know if you loved me. I want to know if you regretted leaving me. I want to know if you ever suspected that anything was wrong.

I know none of these thoughts will help me, so I just have to focus on what I *do* have. I have my love for you. I never stopped loving you. I only ever wanted you to bundle me up and keep me safe, but if you had taken me away I would never have had my own children or my own grandchildren, and I can't bear the thought of a world without them.

Yes, I do hurt, but I know that I'm strong. I know that I will get through, even though you're gone for ever, because I have always survived. If you can see me from heaven, please be proud of me, Mum; I'm special too.

I miss you and I'll always love you – and I forgive you, Mum, I forgive you.

But – and this may sound odd given what I've spent so many pages telling – you're not the only person I forgive. Your mother, my Granny Morag, has been in my thoughts constantly since I put the first words on the page. I expected to hate her when I looked back, I expected to despise her for what she did to me and for what she allowed to be done to me.

Instead, I feel closer to her than ever. She was my blood, I wouldn't be here if not for her. I have forgiven her now and think I have made my peace with her too. When this book was finished, I went to her grave and planted some flowers. For the first time since I can remember my memories weren't bitter ones. I slept well that night.

Granny was as much a victim as I was. No one helped her when she was young and even though I got the brunt of it, there was that side of her that was so incredibly kind as well. I go to the cemetery a lot now and talk to her; I think she knows. What I want her to know is that I love her so much. Despite it all, I ache for her but it comes from happiness and from knowing that it's fine, everything is fine. Life was hard for women in her day, and it must have been awful for her to have lost her first babies – that she allowed that to colour her life isn't that surprising now I can see the whole picture.

Writing this book has set me free, Mum. I wish you could be

here to see how much stronger I am, but I know you're watching over me – I hope Granny Morag is too, because I love you both so much.

I wish I could pick up that wee lassie in the picture and take her home, keep her safe and shower her with cuddles and affection. It's too late for her – but it's not too late for me. I owe it to myself to look to the future and not dwell in the past. I'm not the sum total of what was done to me, I'm my own person and I have the blood of strong women in my veins. I'll face the rest of my life with pride in what I've achieved and hope that we'll meet again – there's still a chance for you to love me, because I know that's all the three of us ever wanted really.

Sheena xx

Acknowledgements

This whole book really is for one person – for my Mum in Heaven. I hope that somehow she will finally know my story and understand what I went through. I love you, Mum – some day we will be together again.

It is for my children and my grandchildren who I adore and who I would do anything for, no matter what stood in my way.

It is for my sisters and brothers in America – I am so proud of each and every one of you, and I hope you will always be in my life.

And it's for Jesus: I'm sorry for blaming you for everything. You were always on my side; I just couldn't see you there when times were tough.

There have been moments when I have thought that no one would ever believe me – but, finally, someone did.

I'd like to thank, more than anyone, my ghost writer, Linda Watson-Brown, who listened and never judged, and who made sense of all of this. She helped me get my words down on paper and I will never forget that. She can have no idea how much it means to me to know that someone heard that little girl from all those years ago or of the change it has brought about in the woman I now am. I feel able to forgive myself and I feel able to see that I'm worth something, and that's nothing short of a miracle.

Thank you also to our agent, Clare Hulton, who made this happen, and to the team at Simon & Schuster, including Kerri Sharp, and all of those people who I'll never meet or know but who have worked so hard to make sure that my story, and the story of others like me, is out there.

Contacting Sheena

I have had to retain my anonymity for this book as some of the perpetrators are still alive. I wish I didn't have to, but that's how things work – the victims are silenced all over again. However, if you do want to contact me (and I'd love to hear from you), please do feel free to send me a message through Linda who you can reach at:

l.wb@stampless.co.uk

www.lindawatsonbrown.co.uk

She'll pass everything on to me – thank you all so much, thank you for everything but mostly for taking the time to read my story and hopefully, just hopefully, believing.